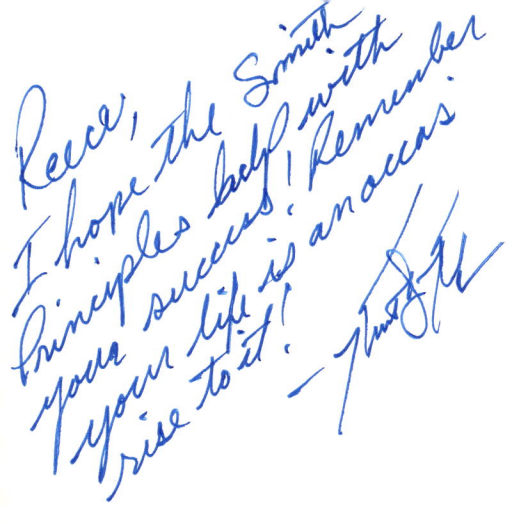

The SMITH Principles
Leading from a Place of Truth

Kurt Klein, MBA

No part of this publication may be reproduced , stored in a retrieval system, or transmitted in any form or by any means, electronic, mechanical, photocopying, recording, scanning, or otherwise, except as permitted by Sections 107 or 108 of the 1976 United States Copyright Act, without either the prior written permission of the publisher or authorization through payment of the per-copy fee to the Copyright Clearance Center, 1847 HWY 46 Suite A, New Braunfels, Texas 78132. Requests to the Author for permission should be addressed to Kurt Klein 1847 HWY 46 Suite A, New Braunfels, TX 78132, (830) 629-5665, e-mail: smithprinciples@gmail.com

While the stories in this book are based on the author's real-life experiences, this is a work of fiction. Names, characters, businesses, places, events, locales, and incidents are either the products of the author's imagination or used in a fictitious manner. Any resemblance to actual persons, living or dead, or actual events is purely coincidental.

Copyright © 2019 Kurt Klein, MBA

All rights reserved.

ISBN: **9781691078158**

DEDICATION

I want to thank all those people I had the distinct pleasure to lead. Without you intrepid folks we'd never have won as much as we did! Thank you for being awesome for us!
I am grateful to all those who loved me. For all those who didn't you were a great example of what not to do, thank you. I'd not be who I am today without you. Thanks to all who had the guts to go along for the ride. I love you more than my words can ever say!
To my children – I'm not sure I can ever say it enough, I love you three with all my heart.
To Matt – You gave me my words in the deadline so long ago. Thank you, brother. Your support and friendship have meant the world to me.
To Mary Ann – Without you, this book would not exist. People come into our lives for a reason, a season and a lifetime. You were the mentor I needed. Thank you for all your contributions to this work.
To The Julie: It has been an honor to be loved by you. Thank you for enduring this journey. I love you. I am grateful for your love.

CONTENTS

	Preface	i
1	YOU!	1
2	WAKE UP CALL	4
3	S.M.I.T.H.	9
4	FRAUDS	14
5	WHAT? TRUE WHAT?	20
6	TRUE LEADERS	25
7	STEWARDSHIP	29
8	MENTORSHIP	45
9	INTEGRITY	57
10	TRUTH OVER HARMONY	74
11	SUCCESSION & THE TRUE LEADER	90
12	WHAT COULD POSSIBLY GO WRONG?	93

PREFACE

This book represents a lifelong love affair with leadership. For over twenty years, I've been working at putting this advice on paper. To teach others, I feel you must have done the job yourself long enough to be considered a master of your craft. What this means is that you had to have "been there and done that." Otherwise, how can you speak with any credibility?

Throughout my entire professional history, I've been the leader, whether I wanted the role or not. While this may seem to be an august position, it is a responsibility few people handle well. A leader isn't just the strongest or the biggest or the fastest. A leader is one who understands the responsibility and knows that if he or she drops the ball, others ultimately suffer. As a leader, I found I had to make my people better.

I have always been asked to get the job done. I have been that "go-to guy" time and time again. I was assigned teams that were lacking. I inherited crews that no longer worked efficiently; they were quite broken. It was up to me to fix them or wipe the slate clean.

I received these employees after another "leader" had run them into the ground by overworking, under-developing, and simply not caring for them. Most of the teams were deemed beyond repair by the leadership in place. I believe I was given these people because someone knew I wouldn't give up on what appeared to be a hopeless situation. I was brought in to recover departments and bring them out of the red. I possess a rare talent of identifying strengths and weaknesses and making square pegs fit with round holes. At the end of the day, I was the perfect guy for the job.

I found one thing to be true. I could not have succeeded on my own. I realized that I had hidden leaders within every group. They just hadn't been given a voice. They were marginalized and disenfranchised. Most had one foot out the door. My resolve and mission statement were the only tools I had. I never arrived leading a cavalry. I arrived alone. For most of my teams, this didn't inspire great hope for a positive outcome. I'm sure many of them felt they'd been handed a garden hose to put out a three-alarm fire!

I made a difference in the success of my people by using the principles in this book. I found that it was not an *"I"* situation as much as it was a *"we"* situation. *"We"* were all in it together.

A solid leader knows that to succeed, they must elevate everyone. They inspire others to greater levels of achievement and success. Anyone who accomplishes that with great **stewardship, mentorship, integrity,** and **truth over harmony**, is a TRUE Leader. My book explains each of these qualities.

What I found was that there were two types of leaders — those who were worthy of TRUE leader titles and those who were frauds. There's hope. Frauds just need to be repurposed, and they can get back on track to being TRUE leaders. Hopefully, as you complete this book, you'll join the TRUE leader ranks.

This book is your guide to TRUE leadership. I guarantee the principles in this book will change your life. I invite you to join the conversations with SMITH.

Author's Note

Pronouns. I agonized over pronouns. Do I write *he or she, him or her, he/she or him/her?* I've always thought that writing cleanly and clearly would allow for smooth reading. I chose You...

CHAPTER 1
YOU!

You're standing there. In a large crowd. Wearing your pajamas. You are in an audience packed with animated, frenetic people. Yet, oddly enough, you cannot hear a single sound. Before you can react to this bizarre turn of events, the crowd seems to erupt in a roar as the first speaker steps onto the stage.

You've seen him before. White hair, regal stature, his clothing is beyond retro - it looks antique. He smiles and waves at the assembly. The next speaker is announced, and you still can't hear anything as the crowd appears to flare-up with even greater ferocity. This guy is also crazy familiar! He has jet black hair. He's tall, and his top hat looks a little "over-the-top." The next speaker is presented, and the crowd nearly comes unglued! This guy looks somewhat like the first, and you have this absurd notion you know him somehow! The final speaker approaches the podium, and the crowd just about loses its collective mind! Another recognizable face. Like some actor who played a 1940's gangster or something. You're sure you know them all.

But where are you? Why are you in your pajamas? What's with the silence? All you can think is, *"how weird."* And, then you wake up. It was a dream. It nags at you the whole time you're getting ready for work.

Who were those guys? Where the heck were you? You think to yourself. Exasperated that you can't put your finger on it, you reach into your pocket to grab your keys, and you pull out a handful of coins instead.

You take a random coin and turn it face up. It dawns on you. It's one of the guys from your dream. You flip over a couple more coins, and they're all there. Washington, Lincoln, Jefferson, and FDR.

History tells us that we are looking at the face of "a great leader" on each coin. They don't put the faces of slackers in circulation. When you look at the image on the coin, you realize that you know a general story about the guy. You may even be able to repeat some of his famous quotes. We commemorate Great leaders. But then, it's easy to remember the remarkable leaders. They are so few and far between.

Take a look at the leaders around you. Notice a simple fact. There's a literal cornucopia of leadership styles in the world today. Some are amazing examples, and some are completely lackluster examples. I've always thought there's a right way to get the job done and there's a wrong way. The "right way" can always be improved upon for greater efficiency and stronger impact.

Think this through for a moment. You've gotten this far. Do you want to take your place amongst those great leaders? Do you want to earn increased respect in your workplace? Your home? Your school? Your community? Do you want to be the kind of person who changed yourself so that you could inspire others and leave them better than you found them?

Today is your lucky day! I'm going to share with you the four foundational principles that are necessary to make a great leader. I'm not just going to give you "tricks" to succeed momentarily in your profession or your life. I'm going to share principles that need to become a permanent part of your personality. I am going to take you beyond average leadership to what I call TRUE leadership.

We just met today. But, I wrote this book for you. YOU are my main character. SMITH is your mentor. If you can fully immerse yourself into this book, the principles inside will add to the fabric of who you are. I promise you'll see success as you master the concepts in this book. The whole premise of writing this as "YOU" and SMITH is so that you see yourself there - learning.

TRUE leaders are those individuals who stand out from the rest. They define themselves by how they handle the situations thrust upon them. They get uncommon results from their employees. They can be ridiculously complex, or they can be exceptionally simple. What they achieve is quite often extraordinary. TRUE leaders use four principles that separate them from their peers.

TRUE leaders use **Stewardship, Mentorship, Integrity,** and **Truth over Harmony,** otherwise known as **S.M.I.T.H**. These four character attributes (or behaviors) allow them to get more results with less wasted effort. These four traits aren't just something that a TRUE leader "turns on" when the situation calls for it. These qualities are an integral part of a TRUE leader's overall character. All the time. Every day. It's not a choice. It's an ingrained compulsion that operates 24/7, 365!

As I take you through this journey, you'll find examples of what not to do and what to do.

CHAPTER 2
WAKE UP CALL

You arrive at work a few minutes early, eager to get the day started. You want to prove you're worthy of that upcoming promotion and raise. You believe if you could scratch your way into a position of leadership, you could help turn the company around. Morale is down because of widespread neglect. Lack of expertise didn't stop foolhardy leaders from promoting people who were not ready. They'll do anything to get the job, and they'll say whatever it takes to keep the job. Looking at the drought of "leadership," you're convinced your influence would be the catalyst for improvement.

You immediately go to work. But, before you get too far, someone stops by to let you know management has announced, yet another, last-minute cheer session. A "cheer session" at this company is code for... Everyone drops what you're doing and experience death by meeting. This one, you surmise, was put together at the last minute. Last-minute meetings are less planned than usual. You're fairly certain you're not going to miss anything important at the beginning, so you go in search of much needed, eye-opening caffeine.

As you walk into the breakroom, your attention is drawn to a stranger sitting at one of the corner tables, sipping his coffee. You feel his presence before you see him... he's a little unnerving. Who is this guy? Why would Sean Connery be hanging out here? Everything about this mystery-man is precise. His hair and beard belong in a GQ photoshoot. He's got a style all his own that unconventionally speaks to business. He's sitting there as if he owns the building.

The breakroom space suddenly feels very small. You get the notion he's never met a stranger, and he's always been in control.
His perfect Zen posture makes you wish you would hit the gym more often.

He looks at you from behind his coffee and says, "Morning."

"Good Morning," you reply while pouring your own cup of Joe.

"Heading to the meeting?" he asks.

"Yup. No hurry, probably the same old last-minute rah-rah rhetoric."

"You new?"

"Not really, but sort of," he says with a smirk. "First day."

"Well," raising your cup to him, "good luck!"

The new guy smiles and nods at you, "Don't believe in it, but thanks."

You shake your head and stroll to the auditorium. The normal pre-meeting hub-bub must have gone on while you were getting coffee and, as you predicted, you didn't miss a thing. As you take your seat, The Big Boss steps to the front of the assembly. This moment reminds you of your morning's dream, except this Big Boss is no Washington or Lincoln, and the "crowd" isn't nearly as enthused. Thank goodness you aren't in your pajamas!

The Big Boss clears his throat and begins, "Ladies and gentlemen, I apologize for the last-minute nature of this meeting. We've recently decided to make some changes to our leadership structure…." On and on the Big Boss drones about the candy-coated state of the company and the changes he hopes to affect. He is poised in a dramatic pause and says, "On that note, I'd like to introduce you to the man who will be the driving force behind our changes. He's here to restructure, redefine, and reorganize our company! Buckle up folks; the ride is about to get bumpy." This announcement is met with stunned looks and tentative applause.

The "celebrity" you met in the breakroom steps up to the podium. You swallow hard. You're a little nervous given your brief and, in hindsight, all too candid encounter. Bumpy ride indeed.

"Hello, everyone." The newcomer says as he scans the audience.

"My name is SMITH. Not Mr. Smith, or anything like that. Just

SMITH. I want to thank the Big Boss here for the kind introduction." He pauses and then plunges right in without a seeming thought to sugar-coating.

"I noticed the current state of affairs here is an affront to genuine and authentic leaders everywhere. By that I mean, the leaders here are neglectful of their job, and no one is getting anything done. I don't apologize for my bluntness. I use simple sentences, and I believe you should say what you mean and mean what you say."

SMITH takes a long, slow sip of coffee to allow that bold declaration to sink in.

You notice that your coworkers are shifting uncomfortably in their seats. There does seem to be a nervous excitement building. Who is this empowered guy? Where did he come from? Did he call the current leaders neglectful?

SMITH continues; "Seriously folks, this is a necessary wake-up call. How many of your leaders are just totally amazing? How many of them seem like they stopped all self-improvement measures the minute they got promoted? How about the ones who seem to care less and less about you or take your hard work as their accomplishments? These are what I call fraud leaders."

Suddenly everyone is staring at the floor or the ceiling out of sheer awkwardness.

"Not all leaders are frauds. Otherwise, we wouldn't be here." SMITH says as he gestures to include the Big Boss.

"Take stock. Look at the leaders around you. Are you surrounded by folks who couldn't spell integrity if their lives depended on it? Are you worried about your career path? Are you stuck without a moral compass at the helm?" SMITH takes another long, slow sip of his coffee before continuing.

"Think this through for a moment; I ask all the company employees present here today and via telecast, are you finding that you are trading pieces of your character for pieces of success? Do you feel like you have forgotten what making the right decision feels like anymore? Are you ashamed? Exhausted?" With these difficult questions, SMITH forces a company-wide gut check.

Before you can recover from this thought process, SMITH carries on, "If your position makes you responsible for other people, I'm here to help you. Too many executives in today's world think LEADER is just a title that goes on their door, name tag, or business card. If that's your mentality, I'm coming for you."

At this point, your mind wanders, and you are distracted with your thoughts. This SMITH guy is scary. He's right, though. Too many managers believe that once "LEADER" is a part of their title, they have somehow magically arrived. The hypocrisy doesn't end there. Many of these phonies advise employees to read books on leadership. Then the bosses disregard the lessons learned from the books.

SMITH is still speaking, so you reign in your thoughts to listen, "The problem is these managers don't have the answers. They might, for instance, hand their employees a renowned book on leadership, in essence saying… 'Here improve yourself,' but reading a solid book by an established author will only temporarily boost morale. It will NOT improve managers' skills unless it becomes a part of their everyday mindset. Know any managers who conduct that lack of follow thru? Think you will be offered that promotion because you memorized a book? Think again!

The reality is, many leaders are just stalling their people. They have no intention of promoting them. They are afraid of being challenged or losing their own positions. It doesn't take long to realize that the leader who gave you the book doesn't apply an inkling of the lessons suggested. Talk about a travesty! Truly a demonstration of a complete lack of integrity! The fraud continues."

Wow! This SMITH guy is spot-on. He just said what you were thinking! He just nailed half the leadership at this company.

SMITH's point is one you completely understand and agree with wholeheartedly. Hypocritical leadership exists everywhere. Not just at this company. It is a societal tragedy that those who are in a position to dictate your future cannot be trusted. As you grow and improve, you provoke panic and turmoil throughout the establishment. Your Boss focuses on undermining you or stalling you, rather than congratulating you all because your personal and professional growth presents a threat! Now you're the antagonist instead of the budding protégé.

SMITH looks out at the assembly. He is poised. Confident. Strong. His perfect posture is killing you. "I've got news for all the frauds in this company! The stress and strain of leadership are about over for them!"

With those bold proclamations, SMITH has challenged the entire company. The stunned employees are dismissed. Everyone is instructed to help SMITH better understand the business. SMITH dropped some serious bombs in his brutally honest introduction. Wouldn't it be great if SMITH could affect real change? Dare to hope?

• • •

CHAPTER 3
S.M.I.T.H.

As you pass through the hallways back to your workspace, you hear people whispering guardedly about what they just experienced. Some sound excited, and some are near hysteria. You begin to wonder about SMITH's potential impact.

Arriving at your office, you find both SMITH and the Big Boss already there. Pumped with excitement, you're hopeful for the outcome. You wonder if you are about to hear you're the next regional manager. Instead, the Big Boss announces you are SMITH's "go-to-guy." He informs you that you will be accompanying SMITH to all the business divisions. You are tasked with teaching SMITH more about the company, and at the same time, you will be observing different styles of leadership and learning from him. The result will be to outline the changes necessary to make a positive difference in the company. Everyone shakes hands. The Big Boss heads off to his next appointment. You are left standing alone with SMITH.

Stunned silence. Your brain is about to implode or explode or just simply melt. SMITH is staring right at you. Holy Hanna, what do you do!? You panic for a second. Before you can collect your thoughts, SMITH hands you his card.

"Here's a few of my cards. You're going to need them," SMITH says.

You stare at him blankly and stammer out, "Thanks... but I already know who you are."

"That's where I think you're wrong. Take a look at the card."

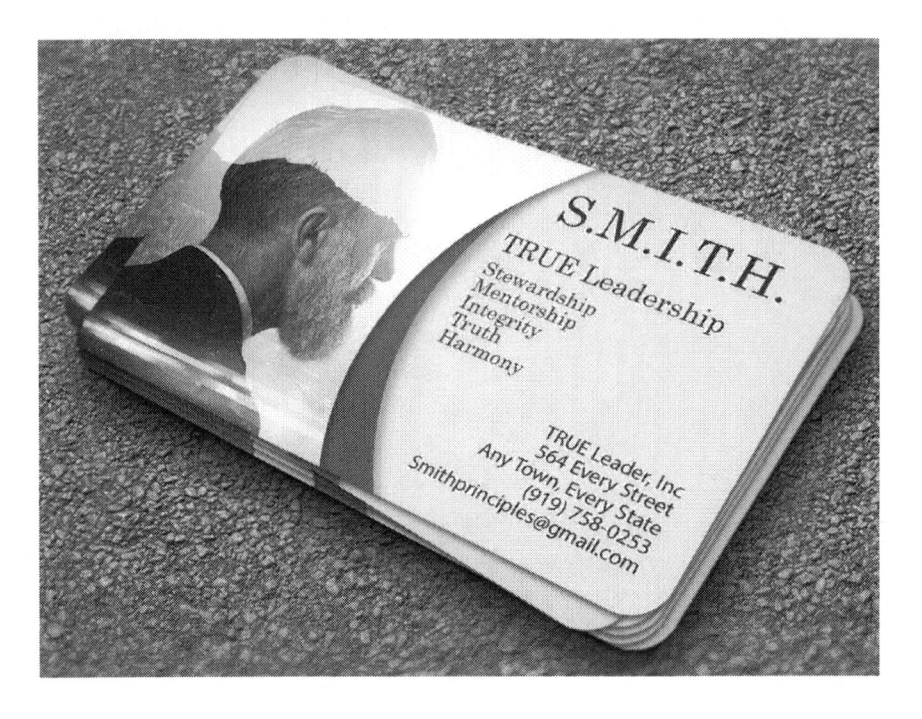

S.M.I.T.H. is an acronym!?

"So, SMITH isn't your name?" You ask with confusion.

"I've been called so many things in my day; SMITH seems just as good as any."

You pause for a second. Then you realize SMITH has asked you a question.

"I'm sorry, I didn't hear what you were asking," you confess.

"You should say, 'I apologize.' You should not say 'I'm sorry.' Saying you're sorry is ambiguous." SMITH explains.

"What?" you stutter. "But I did apologize," you say, trying to regain some composure.

"No, you said you were sorry. That's not necessarily the same thing. The word *sorry* has a negative value attached to it. That value is usually less than adequate. When you use it as an apology, it does little to absolve you of anything that could be taken as an offense."

"Okay so saying I apologize is better than saying I'm sorry?" you ask.

"Yes. Are you a sorry excuse for a person?" SMITH asks as he raises an eyebrow.

"HECK NO... I mean umm, no. Sorry... Shoot, I apologize."

SMITH just laughs quietly for a second, and while he's looking at you, you have the eerie feeling that he's scrutinizing something only he sees.

"Do you have any change?" SMITH inquires.

"Umm, yeah. But the soda machine takes bills too."

"That'd be great if I wanted a soda." SMITH can make a statement sound like a question.

"Take the change out of your pocket and look at the coins."

He patiently waits as you fumble with keys and lint and coins. Palm open, you offer him what you've found.

Shaking his head, he indicates that you keep the coins and take a look.

"Do you think they put the faces of frauds on those coins? Probably not, right? You know those guys as great leaders whether you're aware of it or not. My job isn't just to help sift through the rabble here; my job is to help you transcend from a great leader to a TRUE leader. Once my task is done, there will be no doubt you're the person for that promotion." says SMITH.

Your knees become wobbly, and your mind starts to spin, causing you to take a seat heavily. Did this guy just peek into your brain!? Talk about déjà vu! What is going on!? Did he just parrot the dream you had last night!?

SMITH goes on to inform you as to how this journey will unfold. You will be touring the company's four business divisions. Your responsibility will be to research the current leadership and introduce him. SMITH has been told there are some quality leaders out there. At least according to the Big Boss. But, SMITH wants to observe their behavior for himself.

SMITH also lets you know that you're the "go-to person" everyone has been talking about regarding the next promotable employee. Taken aback, you didn't realize upper management had been watching you that closely. You are instructed to take note of all the leaders you will encounter. Watching them should help you learn how to become a TRUE leader. These regional evaluations will be a whole new initiative the company is taking to become profitable and get back on track.

SMITH says it's time to go home and rest up for the work ahead.

"I'm sor… I apologize, did you say it's time to go home?"

Smith smiles, "Good catch. Not everyone remembers to say I apologize instead of I'm sorry so quickly."

"Thanks, but did you say it's time to go home?"

"Yes, I did."

"Not to argue, but there are a few hours left on this workday." You observe.

"Here's my thought. We've got a boatload of work ahead of us.

We're going to be traveling and working long hours to accomplish our assignment. We should take the time to rest up while we've got it. The last thing we want is to burn-out. Tomorrow is a brand new day, and the amount of information you're going to absorb will feel like you are drinking from a fire hydrant." SMITH explains.

"Okay," you say, smiling, "you're the Boss now. So, whatever you want."

You grab your things and head home. The transition ride-along with SMITH is going to be one bizarre ride. Should you update your resume or find out what this SMITH guy has in store? Mentally, you're wiped out. You grab some food, hit the shower, and pass out. No dreams this time, just blissful oblivion. It seems like just as your head hits the pillow, your alarm clock goes off. It's the next bright, new day.

CHAPTER 4
FRAUDS

SMITH greets you at the door of your office, and he hands you a cup of coffee.

"Hope you slept soundly. We've got a lot of work to do today."

You hold the cup of coffee and inhale the life-giving aroma. You're charged and ready to go!

"So, what's the plan today? What are we doing to change the world?" You ask over-enthusiastically.

"We are going to be searching for leaders who have lost their way. We're looking for the frauds who used to be good stewards. We must restore their focus to salvage their productivity and their team's respect for them." SMITH says in response.

You stop to think for a second. If SMITH's talking about rooting out all the frauds in the company, he might as well fire everyone at the corporate office and start over! You realize SMITH has stopped talking and you're painfully aware he's just staring silently at you. He is waiting for you to stop the conversation in your head.

"Why do you do that?" you ask.

With ultimate patience, SMITH asks, "Do what?"

"Stop talking when I pause for a moment to process what you have said," you respond.

SMITH begins to explain, "You're basically conducting a monologue in your head. That discussion between you, yourself, and the grey matter between your ears is a distraction to the conversation I was having with you. It would be incredibly rude of me to keep talking and interrupt your internal conversation. So, I pause to allow you time to finish your rumination."

Cripes! What is it with this guy? How the heck does he know you're having a crucial conversation with yourself? And now, he's just purposefully staring at you.

"Oh, man, I was thinking again, and you were waiting again. Does that make me rude?" you ask.

"Not necessarily. Were you wondering how I knew you were distracted by listening to yourself instead of listening to me? Everyone has a 'tell.' You flit your eyes from ear to ear. In a nutshell, you're essentially listening to each side of the argument. You are making "eye-contact" with each ear while the two hemispheres of your brain conduct a discussion. Observing a 'tell' can be traced back to eye movement patterns established in neuro-linguistic programming classes. When you get home tonight, take a moment to research that. It will give you an advantage in almost any situation where astute communication is required."

"Oh man, wait a minute, I need to get something to write this down!" you say as you pat your pockets feeling for a pen and a scrap of paper.

As if on cue, SMITH hands you a black leather-bound journal. "The notebook is for observations and thoughts. Do us a favor and save your internal dialogue while I'm talking. After all, if you think it through for a moment, we were born with two ears and one mouth. I'd wager it's more valuable for us to listen twice as much as we speak." He then hands you a fancy, expensive-looking pen.

He gestures at it, "The pen is a brushed stainless-steel Parker Jotter pen. Remember to show up with both items. It lets others know you're prepared. Questions?"

"Yes! Why do I need a snazzy notebook and pen when I've got plenty of both at my desk?"

SMITH sighs tolerantly and smiles.

"I saw 'the plenty' you are referencing back at your desk. Your notebooks are spiral-bound, poorly cared for, fifth-grade travesties. And should you die in a bomb blast, we can use just about any of your pens for dental verification. This leather-bound notebook demonstrates your commitment to the work you're doing. The pen makes the same point. It lets those around you know that you're operating at a higher level. Quality propagates quality. When you function with an elevated mindset, little details make the difference."

"You sure don't miss a thing," you muse. "What exactly was your point about the frauds?" you ask, trying to return to the original conversation.

"My point is that I'm supposed to teach you how to identify a fraud, so you don't become one!"

"I hadn't planned on becoming one," you defend, sounding slightly whiny even to your own ears.

"Let me explain. Temptation knows no bounds; all of us may be susceptible. You or I may find ourselves presented with the right or wrong incentive. Many potentially great leaders will face that moment when no one is watching. They must resist the dark side of the force. A fraudulent leader is born when a TRUE leader couldn't tell the temptation to "take a hike!" Their **stewardship** was tested, their **mentorship** was tested, their **integrity** and their **truth over harmony** were all tested, and they FAILED."

SMITH takes a moment and refers to something written down in his black notebook. Before you can interject, he speaks again.

"Every leader in the history of man, from the beginning of time to the end of time, has and will be faced with corrupt temptations. It is in these moments that we choose to define ourselves. We either become a TRUE Leader or a fraudulent Leader. There is no in-between."

SMITH looks at his watch and asks if you've got anything you need to accomplish today.

"Actually, I do," you respond gratefully, "It would be awesome to finish up some projects before we begin this journey."

At your desk, you're bustling right along, and you're on track to get done about two hours early. The itinerary for the "TRUE Leader" tour is all set. Today has been the perfect workday. You got out of the house on time. You didn't spill any coffee on your shirt while driving through traffic. You didn't get a flat tire. You miraculously caught every green light. You're on the homestretch. SMITH dropped some cool information bombs, and you got a slick new journal and pen. Now, you're planning on wrapping up with some busywork. Then, home to relax!

Unexpectedly, your manager pops in. He informs you that he's got you all set up on another project. You were done for the day. The litany of "below the line" thoughts that race through your mind like a ticker tape is extensive. This guy must be one of the boneheaded leaders SMITH has been talking about earlier.

Your outward display of compliance hides the fact that you're angry and indignant. You had your mind set on doing something simple and allowing your day to wind down gently, but instead, another flipping project! Aggravated, you begin your next assignment, resentment fuels your determination, and you dive right in. You'll show him! You bust your tail and get the project knocked out in the next three hours. New record time achieved!

GREAT! You're still an extra hour over your regular day. Your manager is seriously a real inconsiderate leader! Or at least that's what you mutter to yourself as you drive home. He completely cheated you out of three hours. You're so amped up; you're convinced this was the final straw. You're going to march in there tomorrow and let him know exactly who he's dealing with; you're nobody's fool!

As you arrive to work, SMITH meets you before you can confront your manager. He hands you a fresh cup of coffee.

"That was some crazy intense work you did yesterday," SMITH says approvingly. His compliment is a complete pattern interrupt.

You look at SMITH. "Um, thanks, I guess."

SMITH continues talking.

"Did you know the project you completed yesterday should have taken two people eight hours to finish? You crushed it in three hours! You must have been firing on all cylinders with a turbocharger. You saved the company a ton of staff hours, and now the whole team is ahead of schedule. You know, I believe it's this work ethic that has you in the running for the next promotion."

You look at SMITH and shake your head. "Thanks for that. You just saved me from making a complete fool of myself."

SMITH takes a sip of his coffee while giving you time to reflect, "Okay."

You respond slowly and with a bit of chagrin, "I thought my boss was inconsiderate of my time. I even called him a bonehead in my mind. He saw the bigger picture. He positioned me so the whole team could benefit. Now everyone is ahead, and I'm the golden child," you say, still chagrined with this realization.

SMITH takes another sip of his coffee, "Your boss gave you an opportunity to prove yourself. If you took a breath to see the picture as he saw it and walk in his shoes a moment, you'd know he was working to help everyone. You are correct; your thoughts and words need to be impeccable. You need to use shrewdness when you decide to pass judgment on people. You almost sabotaged yourself with a poor reaction."

He smiles at you. "This is great coffee!"
He walks away, confidently, having made his point. The rest of

the day goes on without incident. As you're wrapping up to head home, SMITH stops in and asks if you'd like to join him for dinner.

You're mentally exhausted; you beg-off for a raincheck.

"That's too bad," SMITH says, "I was thinking of a nice sit-down with some friends I think you'd benefit from meeting. Oh well, next time perhaps. Have a good evening." Thrilled to be off the hook you hurry home, skip dinner, and immediately pass out in bed without even changing out of your work clothes.

CHAPTER 5
WHAT? TRUE, WHAT?

There you are. Sitting at a restaurant table. In your pajamas. Before you can react to this bizarre setting, ten other people sit down at the table with you. They smile and nod in your direction. All you can do is try to pull your jaw off the ground. You're astounded. Dinner is served.

Michael Jordan, Danica Patrick, Babe Ruth, Bonnie Blair, Wayne Gretzky, Mia Hamm, Peyton Manning, Serena Williams, Pele, and Ronda Rousey are all enjoying their meals. Everyone digs in except you. Then you notice, all ten have stopped eating, and they're all staring at you. They inquire about your meal. Instead of responding, you blurt out, "You folks know anything about being a TRUE leader?"

They all chuckle, smile, and nod knowingly.

Duh, of course, they do. Suddenly, everyone at your table answers you simultaneously. It's a rush of words and phrases, overlapping each other. How crazy is this? Then, you wake up. As you shake off the remnants of sleep, you wonder about this dream. What was the restaurant, and why were you in your pajamas, again?

You close your eyes for a moment and try to recall what all these "Greats" said. Then the words come to you in a flood.

You grab your fancy notebook and pen and jot it all down.

- **TRUE... Trusted, Relevant, Unyielding, Efficient.**
- TRUE leaders meet challenges head-on with a level of intensity that borders on delirium.
- TRUE leaders are those folks who know their strengths. TRUE leaders recognize and acknowledge their fears; they show up anyway!
- TRUE leaders set the tone. TRUE leaders accept the challenge to build everyone up to the next level. TRUE leaders can lead from the top, the middle, or the bottom.
- TRUE leaders can lead whether they're ahead, behind or tied.
- TRUE leaders display a level of enthusiasm that makes others stop and take note. This enthusiasm causes the outsider looking in to remark that it doesn't look like work so much as it just resembles a child at play.
- TRUE leaders know they are the high-water mark others are trying to reach or surpass.
- TRUE leaders know that sometimes they've got to make that last game-winning shot, swing, pass, or lap all by themselves.
- TRUE leaders take charge when no one else will step up. There isn't time or room for hesitation.
- TRUE leaders know it's never about them.

Talk about pearls of wisdom! Your dream was a reflection of your experiences the day before. Feeling charged and ready, you head off to another day of lessons.

• • •

When you arrive at the office, SMITH greets you at the door and hands you the anticipated fresh cup of coffee.

"Our itinerary has us leaving tomorrow for our first business division visit. Before we go, I'd like to set some clear expectations."

"Sounds good, what did you have in mind?" you ask eagerly.

"We are headed out to identify TRUE leaders. I have always thought that everyone wants to be a TRUE leader. When I think about several of the greatest leaders in history, I find examples of men and women who were given lemons and they made anything but lemonade! Some of those leaders never even considered making lemonade, because that result would have been too mediocre!"

"So, they produced the unexpected without complaint. Those TRUE leaders went above and beyond despite the odds. They won the game." You state proudly. You know you're catching on fast.

"What is striking about TRUE leaders is their similar response to adversity. TRUE leaders are the rocks that tsunamis of any tumultuous storm crash against. They are the ones who get the call to clean up the mess. They follow key principles which are essential parts of their character. They have the discipline to stay on the straight and narrow. Their moral compass is set."

"So actually, they're rock-stars. Got it," you say with a thumbs-up gesture.

SMITH nods agreement.

"We're going to have to be on our toes. Many TRUE leaders humbly fail to recognize their contribution. If not for their valuable time and attention spent working behind the scenes, the job would not have gotten done. Remember, TRUE leaders, are effective from the top, the middle, or, the bottom."

"Got it, chief. Some will be very visible; some will be hiding in the cheap seats and others will be like ninjas," you say, in an attempt to be cheeky.

"Okay, smarty. TRUE leaders are mentors, coaches, managers, and parents. They could be the old retired guy down the street who worked on the first atomic bomb. They might be the elderly widow next door whose children have all grown up and moved on. They are perhaps the stranger on the highway who pulls over to help change a flat. They can be the teacher who takes a student by the hand and shows them the way to college.

He pauses to take a drink of his coffee.

"You could find that a client who hires you to be the expert is the mentor you needed all along. TRUE leaders are everywhere,"

"Seriously, this is great! You're obsessed with this stuff," you say without sarcasm. "We're looking for a Michael Jordan crossed with the Lochness Monster or the kid down the street." You say smartly.

"Not just Michael Jordan but perhaps Danica Patrick, Babe Ruth, Bonnie Blair, Wayne Gretzky, Mia Hamm, Peyton Manning, Serena Williams, Pele, or Ronda Rousey. Or some random person eating dinner."

"Are you clairvoyant or something?" you ask respectfully.

"What?" SMITH asks, interrupted in his thought.

"Maybe you're an alien or something," you remark. "I had a dream about those sports greats, and they were all talking about TRUE leaders."

SMITH is just staring at you with a cocky grin on his face as if he knows more than he's willing to say at the moment.

Throughout the day, SMITH carefully defines your search while you write instructions in your notebook. You will be watching for people who are growing toward the understanding of their **relevance**.

SMITH has explained that TRUE leaders define their "why." They know that winning is always about **efficiently** making the world a better place. Their "why" is not limited to board members or the stockholders. They can be **trusted** to leave others genuinely and authentically improved. SMITH challenges you to be on the lookout for examples of these **unyielding** attributes.

After outlining this formidable assignment, SMITH bids you goodnight. Tomorrow, the real test begins. You'll be flying to San Antonio, Texas. Rumor has it; a TRUE leader has been spotted there.

CHAPTER 6
TRUE LEADERS

You've dealt with the San Antonio office in the past. In your opinion, no "TRUE leader" has ever raised his or her head out of that place! SMITH is singularly focused. The only thing he thinks about is leadership. How could it be that big a deal? He even mentioned that EVERYONE is a leader.

You log onto Amazon.com and run a search for books written about leadership, you find over 150,000 results. You're pretty sure at least some of those are duplicates, but that's a huge number. You open up another search on Google.com for the word leadership, and you find over 5,000,000,000 results. Based on these search results, you conclude that a lot of people must focus on leadership.

You do some more poking around on the internet, and you're astounded with all the available resources on leadership. You've got an 8:00 a.m. flight and the clock is saying it's midnight — time for bed. Your head hits the pillow like a brick.

• • •

And, there you are. Standing in the back of a college lecture hall. Wearing your favorite pajamas again. The room is packed to capacity. The professor is writing vigorously on the chalkboard. He looks oddly familiar. Vest, crisp white dress shirt rolled up at the sleeves – if the unconventional style has perfection, he owns it! His energy commands attention from everyone in the room. He turns toward his students, and you almost fall over. IT'S SMITH! He's got some crazy frameless spectacles balanced on his nose, but otherwise, it's SMITH! He begins his lecture.

"Welcome to TRUE LEADERSHIP 101! I get that not all of you aspire to be in charge. Whether you intentionally signed on for the job or not, everyone leads someone! Claiming ignorance of this fact doesn't change the truth that you are a role-model. Quality leadership is something everyone desires. While we all intrinsically hope for a mentor to help guide us, no one wants a fraudulent leader! You must own this."

Everyone sits up a bit straighter as SMITH demands acceptance of this truth.

SMITH waits for a moment.
As the students lean forward, SMITH continues.

"Here's the challenge. You'd think ineffective leaders would be relatively easy to identify. The problem is that they come in all manner of misleading disguises. Some are super nice; some are very mean. Some appear relevant and unyielding when they are not. Some appear to have integrity, and some openly display how untrustworthy they are."

"Why should you care? The answer is simple. You must decide these things about yourself. Are you trustworthy? Are you efficient? Are your actions relevant? Are you unyielding in your discipline? You must define what kind of leader you will be.

EVERYONE is someone's hero, friend, brother, sister, aunt, uncle, mom, or dad. You are leading. Someone is watching you.

Become aware of your influence. Make yourself accountable."

Students are furiously recording SMITH's words in their notebooks.

"Strong leaders made our society great. The more TRUE leaders in the world fighting the good fight, the better! Here's to you becoming a TRUE leader!" SMITH says with enthusiasm.

He crosses over to the blackboard and writes the word *ECOLOGY*.

"Keep in mind; leadership is about getting the job done efficiently in a manner that allows everyone to win! It's called ecology. Look it up. I call it the triple win. In business, there is a successful blueprint. Imagine your company has a customer service issue. How does this unfortunate situation become a win-win-win? The employee making an ethical decision wins. The potentially disgruntled customer wins. A shrewd decision increases the credibility of the company. Thus, the company wins! A TRUE Leader is responsible for making sure everyone is educated and empowered to achieve this triple win."

SMITH turns back to the blackboard and writes his name vertically. He then begins to fill the blank space beside each letter.

"In this class, you will learn about the backbone of TRUE Leadership. I believe there are four foundational principles to becoming a TRUE leader:

STEWARDSHIP,
MENTORSHIP,
INTEGRITY and
TRUTH over
HARMONY."

SMITH pauses for a moment and reflects.
He looks directly at you. Startled, you wake up.

You're **dreaming** about SMITH! What in the world is going on? Are you suddenly singularly focused on leadership too? Now you're learning. Charged, you prepare for the upcoming trip. You gather your bags, rush out the door, and forget your coffee on the counter. In the taxi on the way to the airport, you realize your coffee is slowly cooling back home. You cross your fingers in hopes that SMITH has a cup waiting for you as per his usual.

• • •

CHAPTER 7
STEWARDSHIP

"This is your captain speaking. We've reached a cruising altitude of 30,000 feet, and it looks like we've got a nice backwind. We should arrive a little ahead of schedule today."

You check your itinerary and realize you're going to land about 30 minutes earlier than planned. That's an awesome backwind! You recline your seat, take a deep breath, and glance at SMITH. He seems relaxed and ready for an in-flight nap. Just as you finish that thought, he surprises you with an in-flight lesson instead.

"What do you know about **stewardship,** ever heard of it?"

"What, like flight-attendant stewardship?" you ask smirking at your ingenious humor.

He honors your comedy with a little chuckle.

"Not exactly, but you're not far off. Imagine where everyone would be on this flight if the stewards didn't bother to take care of us. Every passenger on this flight is a unique individual with different needs and wants. The genuine and authentic attention to these needs and wants is the central core of **stewardship.** Because people are so diverse, robust skillsets are required to meet their needs."

You ponder stewardship for a moment.

"So, stewards can't use a one size fits all or a spreadsheet approach to help their people?" you ask, attempting to wrap your mind around this new concept.

"The TRUE leader sees two "versions" when he looks at his people; the person they are, and the leader they ought to be. The TRUE leader believes that someday those two identities will synchronize. That will make for one heck of a self-actualization awakening!" SMITH says with enthusiasm.

You pay attention. You know he's not done. **Stewardship** seems like an interesting responsibility. To some, it may seem as if it could be a burden. Immediately, you feel like a schmuck for that last thought… If caring is too much to ask, then your ability to be a **steward** is most definitely lacking.

SMITH continues to lecture, and you briefly wonder if you should be taking notes.

"Thanks to today's technology, we can cut out meaningful relationships. And I say that sarcastically, technology makes quality communication a challenge. Everyone seems to be plugged in and tuned out at the same time. We reach out faster, but our connections are shallow. We have lost our face-to-face interactions and even some of our interpersonal language skills. It is much easier to be apathetic when a relationship is superficial and electronic. No good **steward** can be disinterested and disconnected. Good **stewards** have passion and empathy for what they do and who they lead. Good **stewards** understand that it is a privilege to **mentor** others and consider it a gift. Otherwise, **stewardship** could feel like a heavy burden."

Did SMITH use the word burden!? He must be able to read minds. It's uncanny how often he says what you're thinking. What he is saying resonates, and you do open your notebook and jot down the highlights of SMITH's monologue on **Stewardship**. Is being in charge of people a privilege? You look over at SMITH to ask him and realize he's completely passed out and peacefully sleeping thru the flight.

• • •

Just as the captain promised, the plane touches down about 20 minutes ahead of schedule. You glance at SMITH, and he's sitting up straight with his tray in the upright position.

"Short flight," SMITH says cheerfully.

"Really short when you sleep thru the whole thing." You say, jokingly.

"Right!? Did you sleep too? That's great! We're going to get so much done today!"

While waiting at the baggage claim, SMITH asks you to look up the definition of **Stewardship**. This guy doesn't waste an opportunity to teach.

"According to Merriam-Webster, these are the two possible definitions of **stewardship;** the first one is the office, duties, and obligations of a steward. That one doesn't make much sense to me. The second one is the conducting, supervising, or managing of something, *especially*; the careful and responsible management of something entrusted to one's care. **Stewardship** of natural resources."

SMITH nods his head listening. "So, what does that tell you?"

"The first one is out. The second definition makes more sense."

You think for a moment and then continue. "I like the last half of the second definition. *The careful and responsible management of something entrusted to one's care (stewardship of natural resources).*"

SMITH smiles for a second. "Nice catch. A lot of potential leaders miss that second part. As a manager, what would you say is your most important natural resource?"

You sound confident as you respond, "Since we're not dealing with mining or forestry or something like that it's got to be the *human resources.* It's weird to think that people should be seen as resources, right?"

SMITH seems to appreciate that question as the bags begin to dump out onto the baggage claim carousel.

"As a society, we do a darn good job of objectifying people. Evidence shows us that women are marginalized by this mindset more than men. But men are not immune to the same sexual stereotyping. Anyone who wants to argue this point must recognize that *sex sells!* If you've ever heard this statement or even said it, you've been exposed to the concept of objectification.

The TRUE leader sees employees for who they are… PEOPLE! TRUE leaders eliminate prejudice and stereotypes and go straight to hearts, minds, and unique talents."

"How do we avoid disenfranchising our resources (or people) and see them for who they are and what they have to offer?" You ask.

"Easy. Just put yourself in the other person's shoes for a moment. Breathe it in. Generate the compassion you need to understand the feelings and thoughts of those around you. If that doesn't work, ask yourself, '*how would I like someone to treat me in this situation?*' The answer is never '*harshly.*' Empathy is a key ingredient to successful **stewardship.** You begin by asking how you would like to be treated. The TRUE leader asks an additional question: "*How do my employees deserve to be treated?*" Use intuition to respond to these questions. It will guide you to make the right decisions." You aren't ready for this conversation to end when you notice your luggage is the last left, circling the conveyor belt.

You arrive at the San Antonio office just around noon. The place is essentially deserted. Almost everyone is out to lunch. SMITH wanders off, and you're left sitting in the lobby thinking about the principles of **stewardship.** Another 30 minutes pass and people begin to trickle back.

As the regional Boss walks in, she greets you immediately.

"My name is Cheryl. I apologize. You shouldn't have had to wait. I thought y'all would arrive later this afternoon."

Whoa, did she say, 'I apologize?' No 'sorry' for her. Good job. You're feeling proud of yourself for already beginning to think like SMITH!

"Hello Cheryl, it's nice to meet you in person finally. Our flight made really good time," you say while extending your hand to introduce yourself.

"Well, where's this SMITH I've heard so much about?"

"I believe he's having a look around the office."

"Oh good, I'm glad he's made himself at home. I had an entire itinerary for this visit to maximize our time." Cheryl says, definitively.

"Tell me, what's he like?"

You think for a moment. Surely, this is why SMITH is absent. He allowed you to answer questions, and you get to make the first impression.

You respond with the frankest description that comes to mind.

"Well, SMITH's every bit the man for the job the Big Boss said he would be. He's a mind reader. He knows the questions before you ask, and his approach to leadership is like nothing I've ever seen. You'll know a moment of his time is worth its weight in gold once you meet him. The lessons he graciously shares can't help but make you a better person."

"Wow," she says after a pause to process the information, "that's quite a resume. Well, is SMITH an authoritative leader or an autocrat or a tyrant or what?" She lets her question trail off.

You realize that she is trying to objectify SMITH. If she can label SMITH's leadership technique, she can make superficial assumptions. You already know this approach will not effectively define SMITH. Cheryl will miss a huge learning curve if she tries to squeeze SMITH into a generic definition of a leader.

"Honestly he's not any of those. He's a TRUE leader."

"TRUE? How are you defining TRUE?"

"Gosh Cheryl, it's not my definition, it's his. He's **trustworthy**. He's **relevant**. He's **unyielding** in every aspect of the job, and he's amazingly **efficient**."

"Goodness, you sound like a loyal disciple."

You blush at the description and inform Cheryl, "Actually, I think I just put it all together, we only met this week."

"Well let's go find this TRUE leader of yours and see what we can teach him."

The search for SMITH allows you and the regional manager to take a tour of the facility. This circumstance might have been orchestrated by SMITH to allow you to interact with this executive and practice some of your newly learned techniques. You try to respond and observe with SMITH-like composure. After the better part of an hour you finally find him and, it seems, he has already introduced himself. He's in an animated discussion with a group of San Antonio Office employees.

You can hear SMITH's commanding voice. "Everyone leads. You could be a stay at home mom or dad guiding your children. You and your spouse should connect as two leaders to guide the efficient direction of your household and family. Or, you could be the CEO of a multinational corporation and be responsible for managing hundreds if not thousands of people. No matter your position in life, everybody has a leadership role! You owe it to those following you to march ahead as a TRUE leader!"

SMITH pauses for a second when he sees you. He bids his group goodbye for the moment and promises to connect with them later. He walks over to you and Cheryl.

"You must be SMITH." She says in a nervous rush as she extends her hand to shake SMITH's hand.

"I'm Cheryl, the regional boss. Before you get too entrenched down here, I want you to know I've already told the Big Boss what we need."

Using your newly developed SMITH intuition, you notice that Cheryl is eager to establish her authority. You sense that she wants to seem confident, but she is sending out signals of insecurity. You can't wait to discuss your observations with SMITH. You make a reminder in your notebook.

"Hello, Cheryl. I'm excited to meet you. I've heard tales of a TRUE leader operating incognito down here." SMITH says undaunted.

"Well, I'm flattered to be considered a TRUE leader. Shall we get started?" Cheryl says as she maneuvers to take control.

The three of you adjourn to Cheryl's office. She lets you know in no uncertain terms that the San Antonio region has one of the most organized office structures in the company. She is eager to tell you that she has won several awards for her innovative systems to keep a large office from becoming bloated with unnecessary protocol and excessive hiring. She is in charge of the division. In short, she is where the buck stops.

"WOW! That's quite a bit of responsibility and achievement." SMITH chimes in seeming genuinely impressed.

Cheryl continues for the next hour explaining all the revolutionary organizational approaches they employ in the region and how they are the model that the rest of the company should copy to build **efficiency**.

After SMITH jots a few thoughts in his notebook, he suggests that you call it a day. He would like to return tomorrow and meet with some of the second level executives. He also wishes to spend some time with Cheryl's lead assistant, Julia. He asks Cheryl if she can set up all those meetings. She preens with the pleasure of being able to show off the prowess of her scheduling for SMITH.

SMITH has tactfully suggested a way to learn more about the office without Cheryl's bias. He's so slick! He's a silver-tongued **steward**. At the same time, he makes Cheryl feel completely important while gaining the freedom to make relevant observations and decisions about the office. With that, SMITH thanks Cheryl and you part ways until tomorrow.

• • •

After a glorious, dreamless night, the Uber ride to the office is anything but typical. Class is in session as the driver and SMITH discuss stewardship animatedly as if they've known each other for years.

As the driver pulls away, he shouts a "Thank you" to SMITH for the conversation and the coffee. Shaking your head, you take a sip of the coffee SMITH gave you, wondering how he always manages to get the cream and sugar perfect every time. Outstanding!

Cheryl is waiting in the lobby to greet you and introduce her lead assistant, Julia.

"Good morning, you two. Julia and I were talking before you arrived, and she volunteered to serve as your escort today. She's also going to help you understand our scheduling app."

With that, Cheryl excuses herself to go about her day.

Julia takes charge.

"If you'll load the app on to your smartphone, you'll see today's itinerary highlighted by time and department. Cheryl and I also had geo-fencing integrated into this app. That allows you to navigate the offices efficiently. We recently created an additional feature to inform our employees of the specific benefits available from each department. All they have to do is touch this icon." Julia indicates a graphic that looks like a smaller version of the company logo.

SMITH, Julia, and you begin your app guided tour. You suspect he's up to something. If your mission is to evaluate the leaders in the company, why are you touring a facility that appears to be lightyears ahead of every other division? You know there must be more to this story.

SMITH asks Julia what inspired this app development.

"Cheryl and I wanted to take the guesswork out of our employee's day-to-day operations. The app updates everyone on projects and timelines. It's linked to their social media accounts, and it can anticipate changes they may need to make in their corporate portfolio. It's the perfect virtual assistant." Julia says, quite proudly.

"That is a terrifically forward-thinking innovation," SMITH compliments.

Julia smiles and slows down to make her point.

"I am delighted that you are so impressed with our time-saving advancement. But that app is only effective if our executives are efficient **stewards** of their time…"

"Excuse me, but did you say, **STEWARDS?**" SMITH interrupts urgently.

"Yes, Sir."

"SMITH."

"Excuse me?" Julia says, confused.

"There's no, *Sir;* it's just SMITH."

"Okay, if that works for you," Julia says, agreeably.

SMITH shoots Julia a quick smile and nod.

"When you say the word **steward,** can you tell me what you mean?"

"Yes, of course. For lack of a better description I believe people are our number one resource. The efficiency of our app allows us to spend more quality time with those we lead. Whatever time you spend must be invested in making them better people and effective employees. Rarely do you find one without the other."

Julia pauses and looks at SMITH, for approval to continue. He nods. Julia is so passionate that she barely takes a breath.

"I believe it is important to balance your people. If they run too long without a break, they will falter. We mandated a *"mental health day"* to be taken from time to time. We watch for signs of fatigue or distraction. Believe it or not, the app we developed uses an algorithm that can predict burn out."

"That is awesome!" SMITH says, "What else?"

"As leaders, we must guide with a compassionately firm hand. Compassion comes from understanding the circumstances of their lives. We have to take the time to get to know each employee and then walk a while in their shoes." Julia says succinctly and looks at SMITH. He's just grinning ear-to-ear.

She continues, "I know people are the *human resources* of any business. As **Stewards,** we should do our best to avoid objectifying our people. Knowing their names and employee numbers isn't enough. You should know the person because that is what makes the difference. If we treat our employees with integrity, they will, in turn, treat the customer with respect. The company profits and there is a win-win-win result. We can't lose when we make the right decisions – at every level. Finally, we lead with **truth over harmony**. Truth is always available, free of judgment. These principles have created tremendous employee loyalty. Several of our people have worked here for decades. Everyone is invested in doing their best work!"

Nailed it! It's like Julia is a female version of SMITH. Maybe she's related... But, wait a minute... It hits you like a slap in the face.

Julia is the TRUE leader operating incognito that you're here to observe. It isn't the regional Boss. The whole time she is talking with SMITH Julia has been reading from and writing in a **black leather journal with a shiny silver pen!** It's almost as if Julia is a student of SMITH!

Your heart skips a beat, and your brain shorts-out for a second.

"Excuse me…" you hesitate to interrupt.

SMITH looks at you with a raised eyebrow.

"Do you two know each other?"

Julia looks puzzled, and SMITH just laughs.

"No. We do not." SMITH says with amusement.

"When TRUE leaders run into each other, it's as if we're all speaking the same language. To the untrained eye, it appears we know each other or have possibly worked together in the past. But, that's not the case here. Julia has almost perfectly paraphrased the **Stewardship** conversation we had on the trip down here. You're correct in thinking she's the TRUE leader we came to interact with."

SMITH says this last part with a knowing wink.

No point in questioning it anymore, he reads minds!

SMITH turns to Julia and asks a simple question.

"Do you want your boss' job?"

Julia's face turns bright red.

"Oh, gosh no. I'm not that kind of leader."

"Can you explain that?" SMITH asks.

"Cheryl is a master of the politics of the job. No matter how torturous the details of management become, she tackles it head-on. I'm good with the people. I'm not an *up-front* kind of leader. I prefer to work behind the scenes."

SMITH ponders that for a moment, and you can see the wheels spinning in his head.

He turns to you and asks, "What would you do with two perfectly suited leaders?"

"I might know." You say, cautiously.

"You think, or you *know*?"

"I *KNOW!* But it doesn't sound right."

"If you said it out loud, perhaps we could help you with the answer," SMITH says with an encouraging tone.

"Looking at Julia and Cheryl in action, it appears they are the two sides of the same coin. I believe they need equal footing in this situation. If Julia could somehow be given the same authority as Cheryl, we'd have the perfect situation. But we can't have two Regional Boss roles, can we?"

"Why can't we?" SMITH asks.

"Well, because, that messes up the org chart and it's confusing. Isn't it?"

SMITH nods approvingly.

"So, what you're saying is we divide the responsibility into two equal positions that must synergize to work in perfect harmony. These two obvious leaders will further epitomize **stewardship** as they work together. One is a good **steward** of the business aspect, and the other is a good **steward** of the people. Their people will evolve into an even greater and efficient force, and they and the business will flourish. I love it! Good job! Call the Big Boss and tell him that's what we've decided to do. I think we're done for the day. Tomorrow should be very exciting."

You pause for a moment.

Did SMITH make a command decision? Now, you get to make the call. You're definitely getting valuable facetime with the leadership in the company.

You contact the Big Boss and let him know what SMITH has decided.

The Big Boss asks, "Was this your suggestion or SMITH's?"

You blurt out a jumble in your excitement. "Slow down, man! Your idea or SMITH's?"

"It was my idea. SMITH helped to define it, Sir."

The phone is silent for a moment;
"My goodness... SMITH said you'd have the right direction! I'm impressed. Good job! Keep up the fine work."

Did he just say SMITH said you'd have the right solution?

Excited and enthusiastic that she'll have an official partner in Julia, Cheryl is quite pleased with the promotion of her lead assistant. Both leaders are stoked to be working in what can only be a more cohesive dynamic.

You can feel the energy light up the room with their creativity and synergy. The bizarre thing is, it appeared that they'd been preparing for this appointment without realizing it. You and SMITH bid them good luck and farewell and head off to your next adventure! Meanwhile, Julia and Cheryl are talking about promoting two more lead assistants.

As you get settled on the plane for the next leg of your journey you look over, and there's SMITH already reclined, but alert.

"Just a final word on **stewardship**. It's a privilege to be a great steward. All TRUE leaders know this. We should be thrilled when a member of the team wins both at work and in life. What makes successful **stewardship** so amazing is the ability to embrace the true understanding of humanity. A great steward laughs at the hilarity of life with his or her people and cries right alongside them during painful times. Oddly enough, it is the sad moments that allow us to fully understand that everyone comes into our life for a reason, a season, and a lifetime."

With that, SMITH is silent.

You sit quietly on the plane as it hurtles towards its next destination.

How cool is **STEWARDSHIP!?** Today, you opened the door of possibility for great talent to blossom. It will be satisfying to see Cheryl and Julia win over the course of their careers!

STEWARDSHIP Review

- Your employees are YOUR people!

- Caring and compassion are never too much to ask.

- Your people are the true resource, take great care!

- Ask yourself how you would <u>like</u> to be treated. Then ask how your people <u>deserve</u> to be treated. The answer is there.

- Synergy fosters **stewardship**. It doesn't always come in the same cookie-cutter fashion you're used to experiencing. Keep an open mind.

CHAPTER 8
MENTORSHIP

There you are, sitting at a board meeting. You don't even glance down. You know you're wearing your pajamas. The board is discussing ousting its current leadership group. They fire back and forth various examples of how the team in place can't seem to learn any faster. They even chuckle about how they could do the job faster if they didn't have to teach the slow-witted leadership team how to do the job. They all settle down as the Chairman of the Board, walks in and takes his place at the head of the table.

It's SMITH. He looks at everyone and calmly asks about the state of affairs and the board reports the ineptitude of the leadership in place. SMITH takes all the revelations in stride, and then he interrupts the report.

"Not to side-track us here, but am I understanding you correctly that the people we hired to lead aren't leading as well as we'd like?"

Everyone in the room answers in the affirmative.

"Again, WE hired them, and they are failing. Did we make bad hiring decisions?"

To this question, SMITH gets nothing but finger-pointing at the lack of the leadership team. Then someone points out that the leadership team would be groomed by the board as promised during recruitment and casting.

SMITH smiles.

You can feel it coming.

He's about to shock them all. Then his gaze turns to you! Everyone in the boardroom quiets down, and all eyes are on you.

"What's the answer?" SMITH says as he looks at you.

Taking a steadying breath, you respond,

"If you hired the current leadership team with the intent of teaching them and they aren't learning it sounds like you might be failing as teachers."

The boardroom explodes with accusations and arguments.

SMITH calls the board to order. He motions for you to continue.

"If you're TRUE leaders, you must be mentors. You're so confident that you could do it better than the team you hired. But it's not really about you. It's about you teaching those you've hired. As mentors, it's never about you so much as it's about those you teach. Right?"

The board sits back to soak in this oddly novel observation. A board member begins to ask you a question…

You wake with a start.

SMITH is sitting in an upright position, and your plane is landing at Sky Harbor airport in Phoenix.

SMITH always looks so very pleased with himself.

You are fairly sure that this dream, just like all the other dreams, will be incorporated into this day. You decide to get ahead of this learning curve. As you gather your luggage and head out to find your Uber driver, you ask SMITH,

"I just dreamt about mentorship… Is this what we're about with this trip?" SMITH chuckles, "Of course it is… hopefully, your dream is helpful."

As you arrive at the Phoenix office, you look at SMITH and ask, "Am I correct in thinking that we're tasked with unlocking a glorious future for the people here? When I ran the numbers on this location, it seems as if they are slightly underwater."

SMITH stops before walking into the office and beams with pride.

"Good job taking the initiative to review this location. You are correct. We're here to see a manager by the name of Andy. He has been a beat behind the real tempo for the past two years, and in the meantime, his division is failing. And, you can't convince me it is his fault. The revolving door of upper management in this location has done very little to help develop Andy. He's shown signs of improvement but not exactly what we want. The Big Boss suggested we conduct a token evaluation and then fire him." SMITH says soberly.

"Why hasn't he already been terminated?" You ask with curiosity.

"Andy has the foundation of a TRUE leader. His managers recognized that if they fire him, their responsibilities will increase greatly, and I suspect, expose their failings. They don't want the extra work."

"I don't understand. How did he get the job in the first place?" You ask puzzled.

"Andy was recruited from a competitor's operation. He demonstrated 'Rockstar' abilities and the powers that be suspected he'd be a perfect fit for this location."

You ponder this for a moment, SMITH just complimented you on your advance research of the numbers, but it appears he did a full background check and biography on this guy…

"I'm guessing that **STEWARDSHIP** on our part is going to keep us from canning him, right?" You speculate with confidence.

"Great guess. We're going fill in the gaps where his previous managers failed to help him ramp-up his learning curve. He can become more proficient and possibly save his job. Andy needs **mentorship** to win."

• • •

An impeccably dressed man is standing at the reception desk waiting for you and SMITH. He has three cups of coffee balanced on his black leather-bound note pad, and you notice his quality pen is in his shirt pocket. The cream and sugar proportions aren't perfect, but they're darn close!

With the necessary introductions made, you make your way to Andy's office.

Failing to contain your curiosity, you burst out and ask, "Seriously, how did you get the coffee preferences so darn close?"

Andy smiles and looks at you and then at SMITH. SMITH laughs, and you wonder if you're not the butt of some inside joke.

SMITH answers first. "Andy is very proactive. When the Big Boss introduced me to the company, we had video feed streaming to all the regional offices. A few days before our scheduled arrival, Andy called and asked how he could prepare for our visit. I told him about the coffee."

Some days it feels like you're on the slow boat to wherever SMITH is guiding. You would never have thought to make that call. What a brilliant idea, you jot it down in your notebook.

SMITH asks Andy for the run-down of the business unit's performance. As Andy goes through the highs and lows, he explains that his team was following the core competency's step-by-step standard operating procedures. The team seems to be using stagnant thinking based on ridged policies. This lack of innovation and intuition has stalled their success.

At some point, his team hit a wall, and every employee began to break off and do things their own way, making approaches up as they went.

"We were almost there... If we could get back to our basics with greater proficiency, we'd be over the tipping point. Full steam ahead!" Andy says earnestly looking at SMITH.

SMITH responds with one word. **"Mentorship."**

"Pardon me?" Andy questions.

"You need **Mentorship**. You can read the standard operating procedure books all you want, but until you've been mentored, everything might just be a bit fuzzy or out of sync. **Mentorship** is a 'tell-show-do' approach. Being mentored appropriately, you should know not just the core competencies but the short-cuts that allow for greater innovation and time-saving intuition. Trying to figure the solution to your current dilemma without a mentor is much like figuring out how your credit score is calculated, which is just about impossible for anyone."

Andy looks slightly dismayed.

"Lucky for you, I've brought an individual who can do this job in half the time it takes two people to do it," SMITH says this last part as he gestures in your direction.

Stunned, you simply nod your head in the affirmative.

"Oh, that's all!" Andy says jovially, sounding both defeated and hopeful.

"How long do you think that will take?"

SMITH looks at you.

You step up to the challenge, "Andy, I think mastery of the subject matter typically takes 10,000 hours, which is just about 14 months straight if you don't sleep at all."

Andy's expression deflates.

"WOW… So, what is that in dog years?" Andy inquires, trying to inject some humor into his impossible situation.

You smile.

"Oh goodness, we don't have that kind of time." I believe if we review the S.O.P., I can help you understand what to delegate to other departments to help you move quickly with your team."

Andy lets out a long, slow breath.

"Are you talking about actually retraining me to do the job I've been floundering in for the past two years?"

"Don't look at it as a 'retraining' Andy," SMITH interjects.

"See this as a review and then a preview of what you know and what you can expedite. You'll gain mastery of this approach in no time as you **MENTOR** your team on the intricacies."

"Seriously though, it took me two years to get this point. When I've asked for help in the past, I'm given the operations handbook and told to get on with it. Now you're telling me just a 'push' in the right direction will do the trick!?"

"Should I just polish up my resume!" Andy exclaims.

"You could do that, but I'd wager you'll find this same problem plaguing you wherever you go," SMITH says quietly.

Frustrated, Andy visibly restrains an outburst. SMITH looks at Andy.

"In the past two years, did any of your 'bosses' actually sit down with you to make sure you fully understood your job before shoving the operations handbook into your face?"

Andy leans in closer to you and SMITH as if to get to the point faster, "NO!" he exhales.

SMITH looks at Andy and says, "I understand your frustration. We're here to help. An attitude adjustment might facilitate success. Do you need a minute? We came here to judge whether we should keep you or fire you. Wouldn't it be great if you allowed us the opportunity to evaluate you fairly to save your job?"

Andy sits back for a moment and takes a deep breath.

"I apologize, SMITH, I've been on the front line for what seems like forever with no help and no direction except apathetic excuses, and now you're telling me this can all be fixed in a matter of what…days?"

SMITH looks at you.

"Actually Andy, I don't think we've been at any location longer than a day or two… Results manifest faster than you think. I feel I should apologize on behalf of the company that help was so long in coming. Trust this man here, and you'll be golden." You explain with confidence.

Andy looks at you and looks at SMITH. "Okay, let's get this show on the road."

Andy is in for a treat. Here comes that magic moment when SMITH turns it all around.

"I believe **Mentorship** is the required ingredient. We give people direction, and that process takes time. We over-engineer our instructions, and that makes it feel like we're micro-managing people. The dilemma here is that we don't foster critical thinking and trust is neglected. We try to mitigate misunderstandings by giving as detailed directions as we can. We tend to start with 'step one' and then proceed to 'step 10,000.' Meanwhile, somewhere around 'step four,' we lost our audience. Have you ever experienced this before?"

Andy grins, "have you ever seen the company S.O.P.s for various activities? They even have a 400-step protocol for making sales. Seriously, there's got to be a better way to navigate through all the rules to efficient creativity."

SMITH nods in agreement.

SMITH looks at you and asks, "what is the best way for people to learn?"

You think for a moment, and then you respond. "I think people learn best taking three different approaches,"

1) Curiosity fosters an innate desire to learn and figure out the "puzzle" whatever that puzzle looks like.

2) Autonomy – this allows people to feel free to explore the realm of possibility, thus fostering more results with less wasted effort. No one wants to work any harder than absolutely necessary, and most people want to produce quality results!

3) Big picture or end results - Too many managers and leaders micro-manage their people. Give your people two to four "Big-ticket" items to focus on and let them find their "best-practices" approach to the result. Micro-managing means you stress the step-by-step instead of finding the fastest most ecological way to the desired outcome.

"What does this mean as it pertains to **mentorship**?" SMITH asks.

You think about the dream on the flight out to Phoenix recalling the board members.

"That's just it, true leaders, mentors, find a way to foster critical thought 'curiosity' in their people. They give them the ability to come to their own decisions stating that as long as the end result is achieved, there is no technical 'wrong-way' to arrive at the outcome." You're starting to catch on here.

SMITH congratulates you on your explanation, "Your answer is spot-on, where'd you get this information?"

"Are you kidding me? I dream about this stuff all the time!" You respond somewhat nervously and laugh.

SMITH smiles, "You too? I thought I was the only one dreaming about ecological processes constantly…" he winks knowingly at you and carries on.

SMITH shifts gear a bit…

"Andy, what is the most tiresome or annoying aspect of your job?"

Andy mulls this question over for a few moments.

"I'd have to say it's the constant micro-managing of my people. I'm constantly explaining to them how to get the job done. It is as if I have to think for them…"

Andy trails off as if the big picture is finally becoming clear to him.

SMITH looks at Andy and then at you, "Andy, who hired all these 'incapable thinkers?"

"I did," Andy says soberly

"And were they, viable critical thinkers?"

"Heck yeah, if they weren't, I wouldn't have hired them," Andy says a little defensively.

"Have you ever heard the statement 'we teach people how to treat us?" SMITH inquires.

"Yes…" Andy thinks for a moment.

"Holy smokes, I've browbeaten them out of their critical thinking because of my over-engineered 'guidance,' haven't I?"

"You most certainly have…" SMITH begins.

"You've effectively taught them how to respond and wait for direction rather than how to critically think to arrive at the desired outcome to anticipate their own needs and direction."

Now you can see Andy's true value as a leader; his enthusiasm is growing with the passing of every minute.

"So, what you're saying is that I need to foster **mentorship** by teaching my people how to use critical thought process that empowers them to think for themselves? If the directions I give them help to avoid pitfalls but rely on their ingenuity to solve the problem at hand they'll just about over-perform their quota's every time. This approach should give them the autonomy they want while giving me the results I need to grow this team and succeed."

You realize it's this enthusiastic turnaround that makes Andy such a valuable asset to the company. Once all the pieces clicked into place, Andy was ready to take on the challenge. This guy really does have the foundation of a TRUE leader.

Mentorship Review

- Mentors foster critical thought

- Innovation and ingenuity leverage your team's experience and intelligence to yield the greatest results with less wasted effort

- Asking questions of your people rather than telling them what to do is key, it empowers their actions.

- Outlining "Big Picture" and "End Result" is critical to offering guidelines for growth. Leaving the execution up to your team is what fosters further critical thought.

- Mentors guide the work. They reveal the path.

- True leaders mentor through trust.

CHAPTER 9
INTEGRITY

The sea is pitching your ship wildly. The sky is angry and dark. Lightning flashes illuminate your world for a moment.

There you are. Standing on the deck of an ocean liner. Soaking wet. Wearing your pajamas!

"Is it too much to ask to be dressed appropriately?" You wonder to yourself.

People are dashing wildly about and screaming in terror. You stop a man in uniform to ask what's going on.

"The ship has hit an iceberg! We're sinking!" The man yells frantically.

"WHAT!?" Your scream of despair sobers the man.

"The **integrity** of the hull has been compromised! We're taking on water. We can't stay afloat like this!"

Before you go down with the ship, you wake up! Great! Now you're dreaming about shipwrecks! Thankfully you're not travelling by boat today!

As you prepare for your four-hour flight to Atlanta, Georgia, you wonder how this dream will be a part of what SMITH plans to teach you.

You make your way down to the lobby, and SMITH is waiting with two cups of coffee. *"This guy's a lifesaver with that predictable coffee!"* You think gratefully.

"So, who do we have on the docket today?" You ask SMITH. This road trip seems to be agreeing with him. You know you've met some truly amazing people, and your black notebook is filling up with valuable information. Not to mention you're enjoying the room service.

"We're flying to meet an interim regional boss who was given a chance to run the show temporarily. The company gave him this opportunity to prove himself. He was a hotshot in his previous position and had been quite belligerent about being promoted. The Big Boss wanted to see if he could handle a role with more responsibility. He has shown a knack for *stewardship*. He's a *master* of sales."

The emphasis SMITH places on, "*stewardship* and *master* of his craft," give you a clue there is more to this story.

You arrive at the regional office a bit early. You're convinced your Uber driver was trying to qualify for the Indy 500 race.

As you enter the office, you observe that the whole place is a furiously bustling scene. People are cleaning and straightening. Several employees are assembling what looks like a breakfast bar. The office, for all the hustle and bustle, looks immaculate.

SMITH interrupts one of the hurried employees and asks why all the fuss.

"Some big corporate muckity-muck is coming down for an inspection. I'll be with you folks in a minute." And, off she scurries.

Perhaps it was SMITH's unconventional appearance and demeanor, but the distracted young lady didn't even stop to think that this stranger might have been someone of greater importance.

You and SMITH take a seat in the lobby. A few minutes pass. The young lady who answered SMITH's question just a moment ago approaches you again.

"How can I help y'all?"

Without missing a beat, SMITH stands up and says confidently, "I'm Mr. Big Corporate Muckity-Muck, but most people just call me SMITH."

The young lady blanches. She stammers an apology and then composes herself.

"Our boss is adamant about being on time. We all got here earlier than normal to prepare for your visit. We didn't expect you to be here this soon. Can I get you something to eat or a coffee, perhaps?"

"We're good for now. What time does everyone usually get to the office?" SMITH inquires.

"We're all here by 8:00 a.m. every morning." She says proudly.

"It's ten to eight now. We'll wait for your boss and then grab something."

You take your cue from SMITH and sit back down. You're suspicious that this is some setup.

The young lady nods and apologizes one more time before she bustles off. You can hear her, shouting directions and letting the others know the corporate muckity-mucks have slipped into the building ahead of schedule.

The activity settles. You notice everyone staring at both of you. No one approaches, and no one talks to you the entire time you wait patiently for the boss. Time slows, and your stomach grumbles. SMITH motions for you to grab a bite. You walk over to the buffet and select two coffees and a Danish. As you return to your seat, you notice the clock behind your chairs. The time is 8:20 a.m. So much for punctuality. You hand SMITH a black coffee. He grimaces.

"What?" You ask, slightly annoyed.

"I prepare your coffee perfectly every time, and you give me this?" SMITH says, motioning towards the black coffee.

"What?" You repeat.

"Seriously, you haven't noticed how I mix your coffee exactly the way you like it?" SMITH says pointedly.

"I just figure you're a mind reader." You reply sardonically

"It's the same way I take my coffee, good Sir. Here, fix this." You make a mental note; no detail isn't relevant.

"He's still a mind reader," you think as you add the correct amount of cream and sweetener to SMITH's coffee. No detail is too small for SMITH to notice. He expects perfection in all things. But then, as a TRUE leader, he is given to **unyielding** drive and quality in all he does.

Just then, the interim regional boss bursts through the doors. "GREETINGS EVERYONE!" He booms as he enters the waiting area.

"I'm so glad you're both here today. I see you've found the buffet and the coffee."

"Yes, we got here just as the setup was complete," SMITH responds.

"Have you had a chance to look around?" The boss asks in his still booming voice.

"Not at all. We did talk to your staff a bit. Your employees tell us you demand punctuality."

"ABSOLUTELY!" The interim regional boss says indignantly while adjusting his perfectly knotted tie. "If you can't be where you need to be, when you need to be there, don't even bother to show up."

SMITH smiles. A very self-possessed smile. SMITH seems as quiet as the boss seems thundering. And yet, SMITH's words seem to carry much more weight.

"The military always taught us to be early is to be *on time*. To be on time is to be *late*. And to be late is to be *dead*. Although, I'm sure no one's life is at stake, in the corporate world." SMITH says deprecatingly.

"HECK YEAH! I couldn't agree with you more! That's the only way we operate around here!" He blusters, seemingly unaware of his inconsistency.

"My name is Mike. Darn glad to meet you finally."

On your flight to Atlanta SMITH had explained to you that Ph.D.'s in linguistics have hammered out a rough sum of all the parts of communication. He said the experts agree about 7% of communication is the words. 33% of communication is the tone, and 60% of communication is body language. You made a note of these percentages in your leather-bound notebook so that you will remember them.

As you observe Mike, he seems overly confident. But, he's not who SMITH told you to watch. SMITH advised you to pay attention to the people who work with him.

SMITH and Mike continue their banter. You notice the employees milling around you are avoiding eye contact. Every arrogant proclamation, Mr. Over-Confident Mike makes is met with negative body language from those who are near him.

This experiment is fascinating. You excuse yourself from the meeting and decide to tour the facility on your own.

The regional office employees immediately approach you.

"Did the *Bosses* kick you out of their meeting? One of them asks.

"I excused myself to be able to take a look around and talk with you folks." You say, conveying authority.

"Oh, sure, you did." They all laugh with apprehensive uncertainty.

"Seriously, who's this SMITH guy? Mike told us he was going to *white glove* this place, and all our jobs are on the line." You sense they need to be reassured.

"He's not a hatchet-man if that's what you're implying," you say calmly. Your statement is ignored as you're pressed with a barrage of questions.

"Yeah, but *WHO* is he?"

"Why'd the Big Boss ask him to *check out* the company?"

"Are we in *trouble?*"

The rush of nervous voices threatens to overwhelm you.

You take a deep breath. This must be what SMITH was talking about when he said, *"everyone leads!"* You are certain how you respond will be very important to these unsettled people.

"Okay. Okay. One at a time. So, *WHO* is SMITH? This statement might not mean much to you, but he's a TRUE Leader!"

"Refined older guy? GQ hair and beard? Unconventionally well-dressed with a retro-twist?" Asks someone who had not been in the front office when SMITH arrived.

You're shocked, but you recover quickly. "Yes! That is exactly how he looks. How did you know?"

"I think I saw him speak once. I own ALL his books!"

You stop short. "SMITH's a speaker and an author!? Who knew?" You say to no one in particular.

Someone asks, "You've read all his books, Jon?"

Jon responds proudly.

"Yup! Sure did! He even signed one for me. If he's the person I'm thinking of he's **trustworthy, relevant, unyielding,** and **efficient** (TRUE). He doesn't usually go into places that are rocking. He mostly arrives when companies need to be straightened out and messes need to be cleaned up." Jon's last comment sounds more like a tentative question than a statement.

"Our Big Boss gave SMITH the assignment to go through all our regional offices and evaluate the leaders. After we assessed the San Antonio office, we created an entirely new position. That office now has two regional managers. Our observations lead us to promote the lead assistant." you explain.

"No one was fired. In fact, by making this move, we created two new jobs." You say to offer reassurance.

Then, you hear their voices in unison, "No way! That's incredible! Come on, for real?"

"Yes, for real. We evaluated the situation. Two of the leaders at that location were delivering effective **stewardship.** We preserved two jobs and changed one into a promotion. Both could accomplish more if they were empowered equally! We couldn't possibly fire anyone in that situation. SMITH is unbelievably efficient at what he does. He can be **trusted.**"

You pause for a moment while everyone else is talking with enthusiasm.

"As for *being in trouble,* no one is in danger that I know of." You say with confidence.

"Tell me about Mike. Is he a good leader?" You ask, changing the subject.

You notice cautious glances among the assembled employees. Apprehensive and mumbled comments are all you receive. Then everyone starts to speak at once. You get swept away in the conversations and stories that go on and on. Before you realize, several hours have passed. You can see that most work has ground to a halt. The opportunity for these employees to express their opinions seems more important than any of their tasks.

Suddenly, everyone stops talking. You turn around, and SMITH is behind you, leaning against a wall. He's probably been there and listening for much of the time.

"Come on, folks; you don't have to stop talking just because this guy showed up." You say light-heartedly.

You make the introduction, "Everyone, this is SMITH! SMITH – Everyone!"

There's nervous laughter. Then Jon steps forward and says, "I knew it was you!"

"Jon, isn't it?" SMITH says as if the name just jumped into his head.

"WOW, what a memory! You remember me?" Jon asks incredulously.

"Yes, you attended a leadership seminar. What was it, three years ago? I was hoping to meet up with you again today." SMITH says.

"Oh, my goodness! That's exactly when it was! You even signed my book. How can you possibly remember me? That's amazing!" SMITH continues the conversation as if he and Jon had just talked the previous day.

"Well, you asked me an important question. You asked me what my personal definition of integrity was. Do you remember the definition?"

Jon can't wait to respond, "Heck yeah! You said, **'Integrity is the currency upon which your good name is traded. It is the moral and ethical standard you use to lead your life, even when no one is looking. It means making the right decision for those you serve regardless of your cost!'"**

SMITH seems impressed.

"I believe that's verbatim," SMITH says proudly.

At this point, the gathered employees all jump in at once with comments.

"Jon, that's where you got that definition?"

"That explains it! He's always talking about leading your own life morally and ethically!"

"You made quite the impression on this guy, SMITH."

The conversation becomes more animated. SMITH fields all the questions they just asked you. SMITH gives nearly identical answers like yours. You notice that everyone is responding positively to SMITH's quiet and confident manner. A **TRUE** leader listens and cares about the opinions of others.

In the course of the conversation, you learn that Jon is a supervisor. He oversees half the employees here. By all appearances, the employees hold him in high regard. Jon has earned everyone's respect by being **unyielding** in his **stewardship** of others.

"What makes Jon such a good leader?" SMITH asks the assembled employees. You begin to make a list of all the reasons:

1) He listens.

2) He encourages people to feel important.

3) He doesn't pad his ego.

4) He is the first one to work and quite often, the last one out.

5) He's focused on integrity-based actions.

6) He wants the employees to win as much as the customers.

Jon seems humbled by all the praise. He explains that the principles in SMITH's books are the reasons he is a more effective leader. And, that same advice has helped him to become a better person outside the office.

The conversation continues around improving leadership skills. SMITH lets everyone know he's always available for questions and guidance. Naturally sensing the time, everyone drifts back to their desks to continue the morning's worth of neglected work.

As you walk away, you ask SMITH about Mike. You discover that he had lunch plans and departed much earlier. You realize your entire day has been spent learning from everyone but the "boss."

You and SMITH need to compare notes. You stop at a small café to review your observations. You decide to beat SMITH to the punch on the evaluation.

"I know what's wrong here!" You blurt.

"Oh? Who said anything was wrong?"

"Wait. Something's wrong here for sure, isn't there?"

"Yes, I was just seeing what you'd say when challenged." SMITH teases.

"Seriously, that's not nice. Anyway, I know we're working on **integrity,** and I talked to the employees, and their boss seems to be a *do as I say, not as I do,* type of *leader.*"

"How so?" SMITH coaxes.

"Well, take the punctuality issue. Mike's got his entire office in an uproar. They all arrive an hour early, and he strolls in 30 minutes late. What's up with that?"

"Perhaps he got stuck in traffic?" SMITH muses.

"Why didn't he mention that?" You counter.

"This could be the day he comes in later for some reason."

"Would a TRUE leader stick to a schedule like that knowing guests from out of town were arriving early?"

"Maybe he was embarrassed, or just that focused on getting started?"

"Watching everyone's body language suggested otherwise. People didn't make eye contact. Every time he boasted about a principle or practice, their body language was quite negative."

"Good catch on the body language," SMITH says with approval.

"They told both of us identical accounts. Mike is never on time. He takes the longest lunch. He bails early for the day. Any time they miss quota, everyone knows exactly how much he lost on his bonus and why it is their fault. This guy is a train wreck. Mike has lost or never had the respect of his employees. His inflated ego casts a dark shadow over any of his good intentions. What did the Big Boss see in this guy? Why did he get a shot at this job?" You ask earnestly.

SMITH takes a breath, and you know this isn't going to be a short response.

"Mike broke every sales record the company had. He wasn't just top in sales; he grew half of the sales managers in every region. It's clear from his performance that Mike has the soft and hard skillset of sales. He can talk the birds out of the trees. He sells ice to Eskimos. I'd imagine what he sees in the mirror is a capable and completely successful salesman. He is cheating himself. He needs a microscope instead of a mirror. The soft skill sets – **integrity** and honesty – are missing from his leadership and lifestyle. How do you help a strong personality realize that their success is masking their limitations? The Big Boss knew he couldn't just tell Mike. The trial promotion gave Mike a safety net to fail. The Big Boss knew there was value in allowing Mike to learn what he can't do right now. This positions the Big Boss to demonstrate his stewardship and salvage Mike as an employee. Mike's got to come thru though. It will take a rare professional maturity to step back and examine the difference between what he is and what he can become."

You pause to think about the opportunity Mike has before him.

"I got it. Tomorrow we need to convince one man to take a step back. And, we need to recognize that another man is ready to step up. We might need to express some brutal truth to achieve genuine harmony." You say with finality.

"Your observations are spot-on. Call the Big Boss and let him know we think Jon is the man for the job. Tomorrow should be a riot with all the changes we're about to make." SMITH says as you both head out of the café.

In the morning you go straight to Mike's office and make yourselves comfortable. The receptionist you spoke to yesterday sees you as she walks in and immediately makes a hurried and hushed phone call.

Jon arrives right behind you. SMITH invites him to join you both in Mike's office.

At 5 minutes past 8:00 a.m. Mike hastily bursts into the office. He stammers a greeting to everyone. SMITH is silent as he looks at you. You're on.

You clear your throat, "Mike, we wanted to give you feedback on your performance."

"That's terrific!" Mike's voice fills the room. "I'm all ears."

"Mike, your **integrity** hangs in the balance. You stand on the precipice of great change."

Mike begins to interrupt; you wave him off. Time to level your best SMITH-inspired gaze at him. He quiets down immediately.

"Your words do not match your actions. You claim to value punctuality, but you're never on time. You take the longest lunches, and you're the first one to bail for the day. What makes you believe you're the man for the regional Boss job?"

Mike's ego is keeping him afloat as he responds, "I'm the number one top seller in this entire region of all time!"

You jot that down in your leather-bound journal as you reply, "So, being number one in sales makes you a leader?"

Mike tries to recover.

"My sales statistics got me the attention of the Big Boss. He seems to think I have potential."

"Mike, I don't agree with you or the big Boss in this instance." You say, truthfully.

Mike suddenly looks poleaxed.

"As a leader, you must be a good steward of your people. Their success should be your number one priority. You have to look after them. You have to demonstrate mastery which you have in selling, but the leadership side is lacking. And, most of all, your **integrity** must be beyond reproach." Mike looks somewhat deflated.

"Oh man, I can't lose this job. I've never worked for any other company; this is the only company I've worked for since I got out of school." Suddenly, you realize the gravity of **stewardship!**

Mike is shaking his head, slumped in his chair.

"I didn't want to let anyone down. I've never been in charge of employees before. Everyone is going to think I'm a failure."

SMITH steps in, "What we have here is an opportunity to turn this all around. I think you can save face with the people if you sincerely apologize to them. Then I think you can bolster your **integrity** by announcing you're willing to serve as Jon's right-hand man. Are you prepared to take direction and learn from Jon? If you agree we could put you back in the sales position, you're so suited for." SMITH says as he waits for Mike to absorb this offer.

Stunned, Mike replies, "So, I'm not fired? I can still have my old job back?"

Jon is quietly sitting on the edge of his chair, flabbergasted at this turn of events.

"Excuse me," Jon interrupts.

"Does that mean I'm being promoted to the regional Boss position?"

SMITH nods.

"Incredible! Wait till I tell my wife. She won't believe what happened this morning! You said you want Mike and I to work together. I will need Mike to help me. He already has some experience with the procedures of this position. I know nothing about sales. How can I help Mike?"

SMITH seems very pleased with himself as he says, "You, Jon, will be the example of a TRUE leader."

Jon gets up from his chair and extends his hand to Mike. Mike wraps Jon up in a bear-hug. The tension in the room is gone. The **relevance** of this decision resonates keenly with you.

SMITH looks over at you.

"I know, I know. Call the Big BOSS and let him know the changes we've confirmed."

"You catch on fast," SMITH says watching the two men get to work.

SMITH assures Jon and Mike that either he or you will be available should either of them need help. You make your goodbyes as a familiar Indy 500 race Uber driver pulls up to the building.

As you get settled in your seat for the flight home, you reflect. So far, you've had three regional office visits, and each evaluation has corresponded with one of SMITH's Principles. You've been able to demonstrate **Stewardship**, teach **Mentorship**, and define and maintain **Integrity**. **Truth** and **Harmony** seem like they may not go together. Only tonight's possible dream and tomorrow's meeting will tell.

•　　　•　　　•

Integrity

Review

- What you do when no one is looking is the most cliché and trite example of integrity. It still applies.

- Be impeccable with your word; do what you say you're going to do promptly.

- Always conduct yourself beyond reproach.

- Your actions and your words should be congruent.

- Owning your actions is important. It allows people to respect you.

- Admitting your faults and working to improve them demonstrates the nobility of your intent and integrity.

- Learn to apologize sincerely.

CHAPTER 10
Truth over harmony

You're sitting there, in a studio audience. SMITH is in the theater seat next to you. He is laughing. The director yells "CUT," and the actors are instructed to run the scene again from the top! Then the unspeakable happens.

Your mom steps onto the stage, wearing a mini-skirt and white go-go boots. Your dad is sitting in a revolving recliner reading the paper. Mom struts up to your dad and asks,

"Honey, does this outfit make me look fat?"

You bury your head in your hands! This conversation can't be a good dialogue between your parents! This situation could be brutal.

Your dad smiles kindly and says, "Yes, it does, dear. You should choose another outfit that accents your figure more appropriately. I wouldn't want anyone to make fun of you."

"Okay, darling. Thank you for your honesty."

The audience roars with laughter! Why is this funny?

The director in your dream yells "CUT" and instructs the actors to re-group and make the scene more "real."

The stage set again; your mom appears in the same costume.

"Honey, does this outfit make me look fat?"

"What's that, dear? Huh? Oh, yeah, looks great," your dad says with barely a glance toward your mom.

"Thanks, babe. I was worried it would look inappropriate and people would make fun of me." your mom says as she adjusts her short skirt.

SMITH nudges you and starts explaining the difference between the two scenes.

"Do you know what makes this exchange so potentially volatile? It's simple. Your father sacrifices truth to maintain a false, momentary harmony. Your dad can 'keep the peace' by lying and letting your mom believe that ridiculous outfit is a great choice. The *positive* intent behind your dad's lie is to ensure your mom isn't demoralized by an honest response. He won't hurt her feelings, and there will be no discord between the two of them. The actual *impact* is that everyone at the party will gossip about how fat and silly your mom looks in the youthful outfit. The pretty little lie will cause embarrassment when the truth is inevitably revealed. How will your mom be able to trust your dad in the future? She will eventually realize the outfit was an egregious affront to all good taste. Just wait until she sees a picture from the well-attended party! Your mom's feelings will be hurt and damaged due to the unnecessary public humiliation. The violation of her trust will hurt more than if your dad had just told the truth when she first asked."

You're still confused about what's going on when the director yells "SCENE" and instructs everyone to prepare for the steamy bedroom action.

You wake up screaming!

You're discombobulated.

With relief, you realize you're at home, in your bed, and there's no SMITH, no mom, no dad, no steamy whatever. Yuck! Mentally, you're going to have to shower for weeks! You look at the clock. Sure enough, it's a minute before the alarm goes off. Might as well begin your real day.

You're ahead of schedule on the drive to the office. You stop at a swanky little coffee shop to get two perfect cups. The whole rest of the drive you're thinking about truth and how it will tie-in to today's work.

• • •

You walk into your office and SMITH is sitting at your desk. You learn that the final visit is just across town. Surely, SMITH had a reason for picking this location last. Nothing he ever does is random.

You hand SMITH a cup of joe, and he grins with satisfaction.

"Ahhh, the life-blood of my day. So nice of you to grab the coffee."

"I woke up in a bad dream. I needed the comfort of my morning boost sooner rather than later," you admit.

"How refreshing." Says SMITH

"What's refreshing?" you ask. You wonder if SMITH is satisfied that you delivered the correct coffee this time.

"The unvarnished report of your morning's start. Wouldn't life be simpler if everyone told the truth? Wouldn't it be easier if people could accept the facts and not take them personally?" SMITH has moved beyond perfectly prepared coffee.

You can tell your dream is the foreshadowing for this day.

SMITH drives across the city to the home office in record time. In what can only be described as a dazzling career, is it possible that SMITH was also a *NASCAR* champion? It wasn't that SMITH was driving recklessly. He just cut through the traffic with ease. He seemed to anticipate every driver's intentions completely. He never once slowed on his way to the home office. You're sure that SMITH also has control over the timing of red lights.

Because this location is so close to the home office, it doesn't have a formal regional boss. Just, Moe, the sales manager. He has been hoping his effective leadership skills would be noticed, and he would eventually earn the promotion.

As you walk up to the front door, you notice a very pleasant and exuberant gentleman polishing a few smudges on the glass. He opens the door and says, "Good Morning, folks, please go right in! Someone will be with you directly."

You stand in the empty lobby you glance at SMITH as you watch the man polishing the glass. It hits you. You smile to yourself as you realize who is who, "That's the guy we're here to see, isn't it?" You ask with confidence.

"What makes you say that?" SMITH asks.

"How many suit-wearing window washers do business in this town?"

"Perhaps he just takes his job very seriously?" SMITH teases.

Your GQ window washer steps through the door and greets you again, "Hello, I'm Moe. How can I help you?" Moe is a tall, well-dressed professional man with a very imposing and confident build. Immediately you know that he is different than most of the people you've met so far.

"I apologize for the unconventional greeting. I gave our receptionist the day off. She's got a new-born with cholic and was up all night. I thought it was important for her to get some rest. Normally she keeps the lobby spic and span; I couldn't let her come back to anything less." Moe says proudly.

"Let's get those coffees topped off, and I'll give you the dime tour."

Moe conducts himself with great ease and confidence as you tour the facility. He introduces you to everyone. With each introduction, he gives a 30-second elevator pitch as to that person's accomplishments.

Moe appears to be a good steward of his employees. It's also very clear that this sales manager has a strong level of **Mentorship**. He communicates the business details with great **efficiency**.

After an in-depth lap around the building, you return to Moe's office.

A young lady is standing and waiting by his door.

"Moe, are we still on for the team interview today?" She asks.

"Yes, I believe so Abby. That is if you don't mind SMITH and his associate shadowing the meeting?"

"You said the meeting would be just the team and me, right?"

"I did. But SMITH and his associate are here to help us improve, and I have a feeling that they will have some insights into **truth over harmony**."

Looking at SMITH questioningly you raise an eyebrow. SMITH directs you toward Moe with a nod.

"My apologies folks, Abby here is petitioning the team to join their ranks, again."

"What do you mean petitioning the team… and again?" You muse almost to yourself.

"That's a great question." Moe begins.

"Abby was a leader on the team, and she ran her business unit into the ground while alienating all those who supported her. In short, she imploded the group and ran roughshod over her subordinates and peers. That about sums it up, doesn't it Abby?" Abby looks somewhat dismayed and begins to object but then takes a deep breath and agrees.

Confused, you look from SMITH to Moe, to Abby, uncertain who to ask what next you sit back to consider what Moe just said. Before anyone can answer your mental question, you break the silence.

"So is Abby looking to be re-hired?"

Moe smiles, disarmingly.

"No, Abby was never fired. She brings value to our organization. When I first arrived at this position years ago, Abby was one of our rising stars. She had a truckload of potential. She had a series of events that created challenging circumstances that caused her to lose her way. Rather than fire her, I sent her to another department to rehab her attitude. In this department, we do sales and service I sent her there so she could catch her breath." Moe looks at Abby to continue the story.

Abby sighs quietly and begins, "I wasn't happy with Moe at first. In fact, I really disliked him. He told me I had to own my truth and earn my credibility back with the team. I had to support and provide for the very individuals I had run over in the dereliction of my duty."

SMITH looks at Abby and then Moe. "Moe, what's next on the docket for Abby then?"

Moe's default smile broadened. "Do you recall when we were talking over coffee years ago, how you thought a team interview would ease the onboarding of all new hires because the team *owned* the hiring decision?"

"Oh my goodness," SMITH exclaims. "I recall we were at that eclectic coffee shop out in San Diego right on the water with all the great books! Yes! I suggested that any team of employees would foster a newly hired member's development if they had a hand in *hiring* that person. By conducting a *team interview,* you kickstart the SMITH principles! **Stewardship** and **mentorship** begin on day one. The **integrity** of the team is maintained, and thus, they all act more cohesive. The **truth over harmony** is established from the very beginning because the team knows the truth of the person who just joined them! Oh, Moe, that is terrific! FINALLY, a student who listens and acts with the critical thought process."

Abby makes the connection and blurts, "Oh great! SMITH is the leadership guru you've been talking about this whole time!?" Her discomfort is obvious to everyone in the room.

You look at SMITH, and he gestures towards Moe.

"I met Moe a few years ago at a leadership summit. He's the one who suggested the Big Boss retain my services to help assess the company and its leaders."

Moe smiles. "You have an amazing memory, Sir." (It's clear, once SMITH meets someone, he never forgets them).

"When I met you, Moe, you were hoping to get a promotion to a sales manager position. It looks as if you made that leap. It's clear you're using the advice from my first book quite successfully."

You realize Moe is the reason SMITH is here. He's the guy who has studied SMITH's leadership principles. Maybe you just found your next regional Boss. Hopefully, Moe has a replacement handy to take over his position.

Moe looks at ease while sitting behind his desk. You notice that Moe's office is very functional, but at the same time quite well-decorated. He has framed motivation quotes hanging along the walls. You make a mental note to rearrange your own office space to be as sophisticated. Moe opens a black, leather-bound journal and retrieves a silver pen from his pocket.

These tools appear standard issue for TRUE Leaders.

Moe looks at Abby and then at you and SMITH. "Well folks, the next step is for Abby to face the music in her team interview. Would you like to observe?" SMITH nods enthusiastically and motions for you both to follow Abby.

As you enter the meeting room, Abby looks a touch uncomfortable. Then she takes a deep, centering breath and approaches her seat in the middle of the room. All the chairs in the meeting room are arranged in a circle, and Abby is afforded a swivel chair in the center. Talk about the "hot seat!" The temperature of the room isn't just cold; there's a touch of frost in the air.

"So, Abby, who are your guests?" One employee asks motioning to you and SMITH.

Abby glances over at you and SMITH sitting outside the circle of chairs and motions for you to join the circle. "This is SMITH and his associate; they're the leadership gurus the Big Boss told us would be stopping by in the last video meeting we had."

There's a flicker of recognition throughout the group. You and SMITH get a cacophony of "welcome" and "hello."

The interview begins.

Abby's career is presented to the group by one of the employees. This recap includes all the high points and all the low points. A couple of arguments break out over timelines, but once someone asks, "Is this behavior part of the solution or part of the problem," the conversation goes back to Abby.

The group wraps up the recap by explaining that Abby had broken trust and had hurt the feelings of the group. She had overdrawn the group's emotional piggy bank, and the team present wants explanations.

Abby stands up to address here peers.

"First let me say thank you for this opportunity. Whether this works out in my favor or not, I'm grateful for your time, your attention, and your compassion. The recap of my career is accurate. When you look at it, it's been quite tremendous. The detractors are the low points in my career; they were quite low."

Someone from the group of employees shouts out "**TRUTH OVER HARMONY!**"

Abby smiles and turns a little red and says, "Yes, **truth over harmony**. I didn't want to accept my truth at first, but Moe wouldn't give up on me. He kept insisting that it was me who was at the center of all the low points. I had to accept my truth and begin a new harmony with those in my world."

The team assembled had asked Abby to explain the following questions:

1) What happened? Who caused it all?

2) What has changed since then?

3) How will she be different and better than last time?

4) What makes her deserve a second chance?

Abby launched into what seemed like a terrifically concise explanation. More than likely, this was a product of preparation and coaching with Moe.

Abby, You and SMITH, are excused for the remainder of the meeting as the team deliberates on Abby's future. The three of you head back to Moe's office. Moe motions you to come in, and he holds a finger up to his lips to stay quiet. You realize he's on a conference call with his phone on speaker.

"Excuse me; I just had SMITH walk into the office here. Where was I? Oh, yes. Little deceptions to keep the *peace* eventually turn into huge stinking cesspools of lies that do nothing but tear the team down. Stop and think for a second. Lying is really hard work. You are committed to piling on more garbage to cover up the garbage you just spewed. Before you know it, you are buried in some relatively unpleasant stuff and can barely tell which side is up! You are stressed out. Your nerves are shot. Your cortisol is up. You start drinking and eating to cope. Now, you are as fat and bloated as your dishonesty. Defending that position is exhausting as well as unhealthy."

The voice on the phones asks weakly, "Is this the **truth over harmony** principle you're always talking about? Where did you even come up with that phrase?"

SMITH interrupts.

"**Truth over harmony** is a phrase I would like to see framed and hanging in every manager's office. It is a simple concept that takes a little bit of effort up front to avoid disastrous issues on the back end. It understands that truth creates harmony. Accepting and owning this leadership skill will improve your life on every level. The key is to avoid sugar-coating a lie and living in denial! Everyone appreciates the truth, not to mention that no one appreciates a liar. Lying to keep the *peace* is NOT harmonious. If you are going to lie to protect someone's feelings, you have just taken your first step to becoming a Fraudulent Leader. A decision to distort the truth completely erodes your **integrity**. A series of seemingly harmless lies builds a wall between you and any hope of becoming a respected steward."

You realize the voice on the phone is Julia. "My sales team hit 99.9% of quota, and the sales manager is insisting that they're technically at 100%! Most people don't see the blatant falsehood. I told him this is a 'little white lie.,' and as such still ISN'T 100%."

Moe chuckles and responds, *"Excellence begins at 101%!* Have your sales manager give me a call. Maybe I can help. Before that though, ask your sales manager to write down 99.9% and 100%. If they are technically the same, then they would appear the same when written on paper!" Now it was Julia's turn to laugh.

SMITH chimes in again. "**Truth over harmony** is an expedient way to identify areas in need of improvement. It is quite simple. Either you hit the mark you wanted, or you did not. Imagine taking your car into the shop to have it painted a different color. When you return to take delivery of your freshly updated car, you notice quite alarmingly, that half is one color and the other half is the original color. Did the job get done? Yes. Did it get painted another color the right way? No. Here is where the lies start and compete with **truth over harmony**."

SMITH pauses for a sip of his coffee.

"Some folks will argue that the car was painted because half of it has a new color. Using uncommon common sense, I argue that if you take your car in to have the color changed you expect the whole darn thing to be uniform! In this instance, the truth is the car did not get painted satisfactorily. Misdirections, withholding facts, and partial truths are ways of manipulating the facts. It won't work… Especially when you're looking at your half-painted vehicle." SMITH says that last part with a touch of sarcasm.

Julia chuckles again. "Okay, okay, I get it. This coming week my team has 6 new business sales appointments. I'm going to lead with **truth over harmony** in my approach and help them close those deals. When that happens, I've figured out we'll finish the month at 115% over the quota."

Moe congratulates Julia, and they end their call.

Moe looks at the three of you. "I guess it's safe to assume that the team is deliberating on Abby's reinstatement?" Everyone nods as a team member knocks on Moe's door and steps in and hands him an envelope. You look at Abby, and she's eagerly awaiting the outcome of her team interview.

SMITH looks at Moe, and Moe nods for SMITH to chime in.

"We live in a *"feel good"* society complete with participation trophies and 'safe zones.' This mindset ignores reality to avoid hurting someone's feelings. The cliché that the 'truth hurts' is only accurate when someone cannot own their current reality. If you feel victimized when compassionate truth is spoken, by a trusted leader, you are forever doomed to remain at the same level of employment."

"When leaders lie to their teams to keep the peace, they shirk responsibility and accountability. Lying includes omitting critical or relevant information to avoid conflict. Ignoring the truth almost always creates confusion and discomfort. Lying is like trying to get ahead by purchasing success with a counterfeit bill. You won't buy much. I understand that this transparent approach is not easy. If it were, everyone would be boldly honest, and coaches like myself would not exist." SMITH says with a rueful smile.

Abby is eager to show she understands and says, "But, coaches like you do exist. There is an example Moe always uses. I bet he got it from you. He pretends one spouse asks the other spouse if a snug outfit makes them look fat. The spouse questioned could choose to lie. They are withholding the truth, with kind intent, hoping to keep the peace in the short term. In reality, long-term harmony and trust become sacrificed. Total honesty may cause a little bit of discomfort, but that's the part of growing. Honesty delivered with kindness creates trust."

You aren't even surprised; Abby described your dream from last night (minus the nightmarish stuff). That is par for the course while making the rounds with SMITH.

SMITH beams.

"Very good, Abby. You and Moe are very sharp students."

"Well, if I'm learning from Moe and Moe is learning from the best then we're both learning from the best," Abby says, cheerfully.

"Truth has a lot to do with ownership.". SMITH adds. "If your **integrity** is beyond reproach, accepting the truth is much easier. As a good steward, the true challenge is to enlighten your people. You'll find some employees embrace honesty. Some will resist it. Some will "wait and see."

"Keep in mind, Abby, that when you're leading people, brutal honesty is necessary, but it cannot be delivered in a fashion that tramples over people's feelings. While the truth is imperative, it is important to demonstrate compassion." SMITH adds emphatically.

Stoked by all this attention, Abby looks like she might burst!

"Okay folks, I gotta know, what did the team decide!?"

Moe opens the envelope and reads it.

He looks to Abby, "Abby, you're going to want to save this letter. It's the best letter of recommendation from an entire team I've ever seen." Abby squeals with excitement and hugs Moe before she can stop herself.

SMITH clears his throat, and all eyes turn to him.

"The Big Boss has empowered me to make necessary changes in the company. My report is going to be quite straight forward. This team interview and self-direction that you've fostered here is something we should implement everywhere. I'm promoting you to the regional Boss position Moe."

Moe jumps out of his chair and gives a "woot-woot" in celebration. He sits back down, realizing SMITH wasn't finished speaking.

SMITH enjoys the moment.

"When you're ready. It's your team, and I wouldn't want to step on any toes. I think you have many strong candidates for the sales manager position. Remember, **truth over harmony** wouldn't support promoting someone simply to fill an open position."

Moe nods in agreement. Abby looks as if she's about to burst again. SMITH looks at his watch and announces that it's lunchtime. Moe mentions a great barbecue place, and you're all on your way.

At lunch, you recap your journey with SMITH.

You talk about **STEWARDSHIP** and how the right choice was to expand a leadership role. You regale the group with Andy and his quest for **MENTORSHIP.** Then there's Jon's story of **INTEGRITY**. **TRUTH over HARMONY** seemed like such a natural conclusion. Then, just before dessert, you mention the weird dreams you are having. You find out everyone has been experiencing those dreams! Three heads turn to look at SMITH. SMITH seems very satisfied.

•   •   •

Truth Over Harmony
Review

- The truth is what creates harmony because no pretense is artificially supported.

- Harmony sets the stage for the ecological win-win-win.

- **Truth Over Harmony** taps into the direct belief structure of a person.

- There's no arguing with the truth. Either it is, or it is not.

- Hiring someone because the position is empty to fill a position is not a **T.O.H.** move.

- The right person for the job is the one who brings the truth.

CHAPTER 11
SUCCESSION AND THE TRUE LEADER

The following day you and SMITH sit down to debrief the Big Boss on the entirety of the changes you made. You've repositioned. Productivity is already moving upward. Reports are coming in from every region about the improvement in leadership.

The Big Boss looks at you.

"Hopefully you've taken great notes in your fancy book there. SMITH says you're ready for the VP role to oversee all the leaders you just promoted."

The speed of the room seems to slow down in a surreal fashion, quick to recover your respond, "Yes, Sir! I'm ready to help; however you need me to."

"SMITH tells me you've caught on faster than most of his students and are ready to launch our newest initiative." The Big Boss begins.

"We want you to be our liaison with SMITH'S consulting group to help spearhead our TRUE leader program."

You're floored. You accept the position and begin the planning process with SMITH and the Big Boss.

You write down a reminder to buy another notebook, this one is getting full. After that, your head is in the clouds and SMITH snaps you out of your reverie. "Did you catch that?" he asks.

"I apologize, I was taking this out-of-body experience for a spin. What did you say?"

SMITH reaches over and almost fatherly pats you on the shoulder.

"You earned it, but we've got a few more things to wrap up. I said, some of your peers will think your promotion was highly convenient. In fact, when preparation meets opportunity, it looks a lot like luck. That's not the case. You've been preparing your whole career for this moment; the right opportunity came along, and you stepped right into it without missing a beat."

You know exactly what SMITH is trying to convey.

"I suspect TRUE leaders get accused of being 'lucky' quite a bit. The accusers probably prefer to see the picture that way, rather than admit someone worked harder than they did."

SMITH and the Big Boss exchange a "knowing" look.

The Big Boss chimes in, "TRUE leaders are humble individuals; they don't need the fanfare to tell people how accomplished they are. TRUE leaders are nearly impossible acts to follow. That's why we had you along with SMITH every step of the way. You showed the principles of TRUE leadership. I believe your enthusiasm, combined with the **stewardship, mentorship, integrity, and truth over harmony** you learned from SMITH, will cause everyone to pick up the pace."

Now the picture becomes clearer.

"So, what we did throughout the company just now was promote or empower TRUE leader candidates. I notice most of those people didn't fit into traditional corporate boxes very well. This group should get to a point where they push one another to get better and better, right?"

SMITH and the Big Boss smile and nod for you to continue.

You're on center stage now.

"One TRUE leader's strengths will be different from another. Now we just need to make sure we don't over-structure our SOP (standard operating procedure). That should help us avoid sticking our TRUE leaders into little tiny bureaucratic boxes for safekeeping."

You look at the two very impressive leaders before you, clear your throat and continue, "As long as we don't squander our natural resources in the leaders we have we'll be good to go. We just need to continue to foster a SMITH environment while developing our TRUE leader candidates. What could go wrong?"

SMITH and the Big Boss chuckle and respond in unison "Quite a bit, in fact."

• • •

CHAPTER 12
WHAT COULD POSSIBLY GO WRONG?

SMITH stands up after your last question and hands you a tiny pamphlet-style pocket-sized book from inside his own notebook; it's entitled "What Could Possibly Go Wrong."

At this point, nothing about the enigmatic man surprises you. He shakes hands with you and the Big Boss and bids you both, good-bye for now.

You open up SMITH's pocket-sized pamphlet, and you realize it is a personalized book of sorts.

What could possibly go wrong?

Once promoted, you should remember that a position of leadership includes a temptation that can be brutal to the ego. If an ego becomes over-inflated to the point of self-centered-self-importance, it will spoil most successes. Humility is the key.

Since we don't live in a perfect world, a lot could go wrong. My crystal ball is broken, or I'd tell you all about the craziness that is going to happen to throw you off course. I've made a list of the things or events I think will block your path to TRUE Leadership. These obstacles are not unique; they will have to be dealt with by every single TRUE Leader.

FEAR. *False Events Appearing Real.* Fear is a stifling emotion that may get in the way of every TRUE Leader's progress. It is your imagination that gives fear its power. Remember the acronym. The events are false and yet they appear real. That's basically a lie; a lie that will sap your energy and drive. Stay focused. Do not allow fear to sabotage your results!

VOICES IN YOUR HEAD. At the end of the day, it isn't a question of, "Do you hear a voice in your head?" It's a question of how many voices do you hear? While you might get a chuckle out of that, it is a reality. There will be voices from your past and your present and possibly your future inside your head. They'll be telling you that you are able, and they'll be telling you that you are not.

Just take a deep breath. You will be okay. The person who thinks he will succeed is usually right. The person who believes he will fail is usually correct.

Have confidence in your capability. Ignore the negative voices. Speak success to yourself.

BURNOUT! It happens to all of us at some point. You wake up one day, and your reserves are depleted. You are apathetic because you neglected yourself. You forgot to recharge your batteries. Your mind, your body, and your spirit are out of balance. Don't sweat the small stuff. Take time to hit the refresh key. I suggest you find your own way to reenergize. Schedule time for revitalizing. Try regular exercise or start a hobby. Without energy, you won't be efficient. TRUE leaders just don't allow that to happen!

SEX, LIES, AND VIDEOTAPE! Sex scandals are highly destructive to teams. The average staff isn't mature enough to understand love in the workplace. TRUE leaders will inspire employees to become enamored with them. Having an affair is one of the surest ways to dis-credit your hard-earned integrity. Office romances create a distrustful environment. Confidence in fairness and impartiality is threatened. Affairs are perceived as a lie, whether that was the intention or not. TRUE leaders can't afford the appearance of favoritism. An inappropriate liaison will cast a long shadow over a stellar reputation.

I am pretty sure there are more "go-wrongs" out there, these just seem like the big picture ones to focus on.

• • •

Thought-Provoking Thoughts

In my philosophical musings, I sit from time to time and think about the insanity that has replaced common sense. Some of the advice I have listened to was just terrible. Keep in mind; you can learn from a garbage leader just as well as you can learn from a TRUE leader. Both have value. The difference is one teaches you what not to do. The TRUE leader leaves you more intelligent than when you first met.

1. *Think things through for a moment.* I've said this many times. It has merit. Passion is appropriate when you're with someone you love or when you plan toward your hopes and dreams. Passion applied to a rash thought or action could be dangerous. You will damage your employees and your career as well. The cliché that cool heads prevail is an absolute truth. This doesn't mean you have to *drag your feet* with all decisions. Just take a few moments. Consider the impact of your choices in five minutes, five hours, five days, weeks, months, or even years. If you

practice this prudence regularly, you'll have fewer disasters to clean up.

2. *Numbers hide problems* – Just because a team is hitting their profit margins doesn't mean they are doing well. Cutting corners never creates long term growth or profitability.

3. *Impossible.* It seems like a daunting word. People allegedly more experienced and wiser than we are proclaim that something is impossible because they couldn't achieve it. They imply what you have just proposed is NOT possible. They are fools. They have allowed failure to kick them one too many times. It has knocked them down and kept them down. Look at the word again! *Impossible.* I prefer to think that word is just missing some punctuation! *I'm Possible!* Same letters. I just added a space and an apostrophe! *I'm possible* opens the world to a limitless potential that allows you to realize your dreams. Make other folks sit back in awe!

4. *FEAR.* This one needs to be reiterated because it is that big of a deal. It is a simple acronym. *F*alse *E*vents *A*ppearing *R*eal or *F*uture *E*vents *A*ppearing *R*eal. Don't allow your imagination to make fear your reality. Those limitations are in your head! Let it go! Stop defending it! Ultimately, it is your *FEAR* that holds you back. Just repeat after me, "No worries! I'm doing this. And I'm going to win!" No more fear, right? Get off your complacency and go be great!

5. *Dreams are there for a reason.* The key is our willingness to surrender who we are today to become who we will be tomorrow. Meet the demands necessary to make them a reality.

6. *Life is like a pencil.* Seems silly, right? You start all fresh and new and full of potential. Then someone takes a sharpener to you. You become pointed, and your graphite is shiny. You're ready for work now! Bring on the paper because you got some awesomeness to create and record! As you go, you get a little

dull, and those crisp, clean, sharp letters are a little thicker. You visit the sharpener again, and you're back in business. You go through a series of turns where you are sharp and on point to slightly rounded and dulled. While you enjoy this existence with the peaks and the valleys, you must know that your time is limited. You started so very tall and so full of potential. You are no less filled with possibilities, but you do begin to shrink from existence. Until you hit that eraser, you've got to make the most of what you've got. Get to the point! So be as efficient, exact, and concise as you are able.

Final Thoughts

One of the most impactful quotes of all time is, "Your life is an occasion, rise to it!" Think about that for a moment. Every one of us was put into existence to do something great. The key is recognizing and humbly accepting the fact that we can all be TRUE leaders. I wish you great success.
 -SMITH

You sit back and reflect for a moment. This part of your journey has been a complete whirlwind. You're just getting started. Suddenly, the Big Boss invites you to follow him to your new office and instructs you to get settled in.

Tomorrow you start casting for your assistant and the real work begins. As you begin transferring files from your old desk to your new desk, you find a copy of SMITH's book entitled "The TRUE Leader" in your top center drawer. Next to that book is a brand-new notebook and ink refills for your snazzy pen. There's a post-it written in SMITH's hand that says, *"Good Luck!"* You chuckle and nod as you say quietly, "Don't believe in it, but thanks."

THE END!

SMITH WILL RETURN!

☺

ABOUT THE AUTHOR

Kurt Klein holds an MBA in Global Management. In the more than 30 years he's been in the workforce he's been in a leadership position nearly the whole time. While he has led multi-million-dollar sales teams to exceed quotas by as much as 300% he'll tell you his greatest accomplishments are his children and his marriage to his wife Julie. Aside from that, the accomplishments he loves most is the life-long friendships he's made along the way. The lives he's changed and the lives he's saved have been what it's all about. Currently Kurt is working on several books, a distillery, and a wellness company.
Kurt lives with his wife Julie and their truly amazing five dogs in the hill country of Texas. Born and raised in Illinois, Kurt has lived all over the United States working with various companies.
Kurt can be reached for consultations at
smithprinciples@gmail.com
follow us on Facebook at fb.me/smithprinciples

Made in the USA
Coppell, TX
18 December 2019